Acknowledgements

This collection of reminiscences resulted from the 2002 Isleworth Remembered event arranged by The Isleworth Society. Inspired by national Local History Week, it was sponsored by the Rugby Football Union.

During that May week, interviews were conducted by, Mary Bickle, Mary Brown, Kevin Brown, Helen Cooper, Christine Diwell, Peter Downes, Mary Downes, Keith Johnson, Marilyn Larden and Brian Pett, to whom many thanks are due. Editing was undertaken by Christine Diwell, supported by Pam Booth, Peter Downes and Mary Downes. Special thanks go to all those who willingly provided photographs, memorabilia and, often distant, memories of life in Isleworth during the 20th century. Lack of space has prevented use of all contributions but it is the fervent hope in the course of time to use further material in a sequel.

First published in Great Britain 2003 by the Isleworth Society
2 Lynton Close, Isleworth, TW7 7ET
with funding provided through an Awards for All Lottery grant
and a generous donation from the Rugby Football Union, Twickenham.

Layout and cover by Graham Hewison, Isleworth. graham@jmgmixedmedia.co.uk
Printed by The Joss Press, 560 London Road, Isleworth
ISBN. 0-9545901-0-4

RUGBY FOOTBALL UNION

AWARDS
FOR ALL

Dedicated to all those who have enjoyed living in Isleworth. Not least, the late Ken Bunce and Arthur Horwood who did so much to ensure Isleworth Public Hall's continued role as a centre for community activities.

Source Material Publications:

The Way We Were – Gumley House Convent School 1841-1991, A Collection of Reminiscences
A Short History of Gumley House 1841-1991, 150th Anniversary FCJ Convent & School
The Story of St. Francis of Assisi Church, Robert M Black
Borough of Heston & Isleworth Education Week, 1936 Souvenir Handbook
A History of Isleworth Grammar School, Ronald Hyam
Key of the Fields – The Lobjoits and Covent Garden Market, Jessie Lobjoit Collins
The First 200 Years of The Green School 1796-1996
Isleworth/Duke of Northumberland's River – A Guide and Some History
Brentford & Isleworth Friends Meeting House 1785-1985, a Local Quaker History, edited by Joan Wilding
Sundial, All Saints Church Parish Magazines, editor Ken Cooper, and subsequently, Lynne Reeves
History of South Street Isleworth, Middlesex Chronicle Newspapers
Historical Isleworth, Smallberry Green School
Isleworth Citizen 1924-32
Isleworth Blue School, Gillian Morris

The Rt Hon the Lord Gilmour of Craigmillar

The Ferry House
Park Road
Old Isleworth TW7 6BD

April 2003

Isleworth Remembered

Margaret Rutherford, the renowned actress, lived in Church Street, Elizabeth Taylor and Richard Burton dined at the London Apprentice and musician Freddie Mercury studied A level art at the Polytechnic. Scenes from the Beatle's A Hard Day's Night were shot at Thornbury Playing Fields, while Humphrey Bogart appeared covered in leeches at Isleworth Studios for the award winning film The African Queen.

Isleworth's history over the last one hundred years, as in the centuries before, is hugely diverse. In living memory people have seen, first the blossom filled orchards, and then household name workplaces, transformed into homes and public parks. Important buildings have either vanished or been replaced. Ferry House was largely destroyed by bombing, but then re-built.

Behind us are the days when children learned to swim in the river or the cockroach infested pool at the Public Hall. No longer do huge barges deliver coal and timber, taking away the locally made flour and beer. But the one constant is the warmth of the people who enjoy living in this Thameside village.

For National Local History Week 2002, the Isleworth Society conceived the idea of capturing the memories of those aged "eight to eighty". The week of events was an overwhelming success. Everyone who attended seemingly had a tale to tell. The result is this fascinating collection of reminiscences. I hope it will now act as a catalyst for others to cast minds back, look in diaries, dust off old photographs and record further memories of times past for us, and our successors, to share.

President
The Isleworth Society

Isleworth Remembered

chapter one
Going Shopping

In South Street

"When I was about five years old I would walk with my mother to Parker's Stores, which was quite a trot from where we lived. Mother brought a list of groceries with her and *we'd both sit on chairs* while she read out her order, which was promptly written into Mrs. Parker's book – every item being priced exactly. There was never any doubt what two pounds of sugar or half-a-pound of tea cost. A carbon copy of the order was given to the customer, who was then required to have the exact money ready when the 'boy' delivered next day." *Grace Cousins*

During the '20s, F.C. Parker, the grocer, was to be found at No.77, while Balch's butcher shop was at 74. Frank Winterborne recalls dozens of sheep being driven down a passageway to the slaughter house at the rear. And, because the mill did not seem very safety conscious, concern about the mule train bringing gunpowder along South Street to be loaded on to barges. The mules had copper shoes and a man followed the wagon to keep children off.

"In Mr. Parker's grocer shop you would see your tea, sugar, biscuits and all such goods weighed up and packed in front of you. Next door was Mr. Lovegrove, the greengrocer, further along *the notable piano shop, Costloe*. Then there was Mr. White, the jeweller and clock mender – such a gentleman. We had three draper shops, Coe, Davies and Gills, where you could buy so many materials by the yard as low as 11¾d and a packet of pins usually for the odd farthing." *Mrs. E.Woodland*

"C. Woods, typical village sweet shop, sold large slabs of toffee some made in

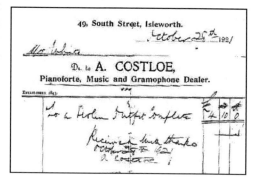

a factory alongside Brentford Bridge. The shop also sold large ropes of liquorice, gobstoppers, monkey nuts, Spanish wood, and *lotus bean pods for chewing*. If the boiled sweets in the jars stuck together, then the mass was attacked with a large spoon. One kind was known as 'chloroform tablets' and were sucked with a sense of danger." *Tommy White*

This shop, opening hours 8.00am-8.00pm, was considered the best of the seven shops selling sweets in the South Street area.

"I was born 1912 at my father's butcher shop, 21 South Street. My brother George Arthur and my sister, Clare Emily, took over the sweet shop at 8a from Mrs Surguy. After Clare's marriage it became Fielders." *John Beal*

"Among several butchers was the Cox family who were at different addresses in South Street for about a hundred years. Mr. and Mrs. Cox will be remembered for the *free soup* they gave away in the '20s. Sunday and Monday were always spent preparing and boiling the odd bits of meat in a copper. Mid-day Tuesdays the resulting brew was distributed piping hot to those queuing with their jugs." *Tommy White*

"There was a pawnshop used by the poor to take oddments on a Monday and receive a small amount of money till Friday when you could reclaim your clothes etc. A neighbour once asked me to go on an errand to the chemist. When I reached it, what did I see but some *cows and sheep* blocking the roadway outside. I was so frightened I ran all the way home." *Laura Hubbard*

"My father took over the hairdresser shop previously run by a Mr. Dennis at No. 25 in 1910. I was born in 1916. Regarding shops at this time, we had Beal's the butcher next door, a few shops along Bidgood's wet and fried fish shop (a tuppenny piece and a pennyworth of chips – a good meal). A little further down Tucker's the pawn brokers were an essential service when

2

temporarily hard up. Just past this was Pogson's Radio Shop. His son was a well known saxophonist in the BBC Dance Band of Jack Payne."

"Going the other way up from my father's shop, we had almost opposite Chapman's the bakers who, in addition to baking their own products, cooked the Pease Pudding and Faggots every Friday night for Cox's the butcher further along. They sent two of their employees to fetch the two large trays and carry them on their shoulders along the street."

"The workshop on the opposite corner of Worple Road to the King's Arms used to be a forge. I often helped the farrier by pumping the bellows while he was shoeing the horses and can still smell the burning hoofs."

"Taylor's the oil shop on the corner of Algar Road are of course very old established as was Costloe's further along. Almost opposite was Fyson the butcher, which had a slaughterhouse at the back. In the old days a small herd of cattle came along to it from the Twickenham Road. And woe betide anyone nearby who left a front door open as many a time the cows came inside." *Arthur Wenden*

Many of the small shops still flourishing in the 1920s, were condemned a decade later by a council scheme to widen and straighten the street. This did not take place until the late '50s when the beautiful arc lamp standards disappeared. South Street was the first to have electric lighting. Children used to gather round to watch a man open a door in the base, take out a large crank key, wind down the lamp to the ground, and change the carbon sticks.

A 1934 advertisement in the Isleworth Parish magazine boasted 'Permanent waving from 15/-. Manicure, face massage, mud pack, eyebrows shaped, high class beauty culture, moderate charges. Perm Clubs held'. While another, at 17 South Street, advertised 'Permanent Waving our own system 10/- fully guaranteed – unlimited curlers'. *Mary Brown, Sundial Parish Magazine*

Also during the '30s Chapman & Son, established for over 120 years, claimed their electric machine bakery produced "The Finest Bread from the Finest Wheaten Flour only". Leslie Wrangles remembers going to Chapman's for one pennyworth of stale cakes – you received a full bag!

"There was a laundry in South Street. You went down the side with your dirty washing and collected the clean in neat parcels on Saturday morning." *Josie Best*

"We lived over the shop at 24 South Street for eight years because my first husband worked for Mr. Goddard, the cobbler." *Sheila Hance*

"I was able to explore the shops after school. Naturally for basic foods we were registered in Cranford but one could spend their 'points' anywhere. At times I visited Coates, the printers, when mum wanted jobs done for the various charities in which she was interested." *Lorna Newman*

South Street formerly had 28 kinds of retail shops. Today it has 17 with grocers, pubs and cleaners and launderettes leading with three each. L. Dennis, January 1962, Middlesex Chronicle

"We moved into Worple Road May 1968. Within a day or so I went to Taylor's the ironmongers for something essential. There was a choice and even though the shop didn't know us at all they said, "*take both kinds* and bring the one you don't need back". So trusting, it gave a good feeling." *Shirley Bascran*

Sunvil Travel opened its new head offices at 7&8 Upper Square on the 1st July 1981. It was "love at first sight" for proprietor Leon Josephides and partner John de Parthog, even though others like Oliver Reed, the actor, were in the running for the premises. Sundial Parish Magazine, 1982

"My first introduction to community life came from the 'information office', namely the Post Office; Robert and Jane Parker invited me to a summer drinks' party where I met many locals. Even though I didn't know anyone here when I came, I've never regretted the move to Isleworth, everyone was so friendly." *Pam Booth*

"At one time there were 70 shops, almost all the owners lived on the premises. Today

4

they are down to 25 mainly lock-up shops." *Tommy White, 1989*

In 1942, Clifford Self and wife Florence took over Coates Print Works at No. 53 from Sidney Coates. Son Charlie joined later and still runs the business. He recalls: "the chemist was Morrell and Howells before Mr. Curd came next door. On the other side was Kearley & Tonge, general grocers - all three premises built by Mr. Wisdom, though Balch the butcher owned ours. In the living quarters used to be a kitchen range with a water tank - when it was taken out workmen took down the bracket holding the tank, and the parallel tank in the grocer shop also fell down!"

Local Post Master, Robert Parker received an award for gaining second place in a competition to find the most popular sub-Postmaster in the London South East Region. 5000 Post Offices were involved. Sundial Parish Magazine, July 1994

Poetic Memories
Dapper Ravenhill, the tailor, grey spats, bow tie,
Sews in his window, you must not stop as you go by.
Auntie Butler the artist, who paints her dog yellow,
Old Spencer – with his vegetable cart – a Labour fellow.

Nuttalls and Browns, Simpson and Woods,
Sweets, toys, Vantas drinks, Woodbines, fancy goods.
Rubber works, Blacklead factory, Coates the printer,
Rowles the chimney sweep, Goddards shoemaker and mender.

Costloe's pianos, and gramophones with horns.
Not to forget the yard of the Winterbornes.
Richards the chemist – clever but stutters a lot,
Coes, Aldridges, Gills all drapers, and old Dr. Scott.
Extract from Village Life – Isleworth in the Early 1900s by Gertrude Sanders

Uncovered during recent renovation - but A. Daley? Surely not!

Other roads, other times

"The Post Office I remember was always at the corner of Talbot Road. At school they issued *little forms with 12 squares on*. If you wanted to join they gave you one and with your Saturday penny you bought a stamp and stuck it on. When you had twelve on the card you took it to the Post Office." *Laura Hubbard*

"During the week the cows would be seen so often going through the streets to be milked, and *the two Bodger brothers* driving them were such portly old gentlemen one could never forget them. Mrs. Bodger, who used to run the dairy shop, was such a fine built person." *Mrs. E. Woodland*

"At age 12 I worked Saturdays and some evenings at Cleaver's in Richmond Road. Used to push a barrow and deliver firewood, oil, etc for five shillings a week. Then went to Riminton, newsagents in Talbot Road delivering papers and got *a one shilling rise*. A lot of people only think of Riminton as only being in South Street but his son had one in Talbot Road." *Eric Brown*

"At the top end of the Town School field was a large pair of gates leading to Linkfield Road. *I remember*

6

the Chinaman and his general goods' shop selling half penny toys and fireworks. Baxter's was a convenient sweet shop on the corner of Wood Land and London Road. My

favourites were either multi-coloured gob stoppers or Barrett's liquorice straws with a sherbet dip." *Brian Cullum*

"J. Balch, butcher, moved to 221 Twickenham Road in the 1920s. The shop was so small the meat had to be kept in a cellar and access obtained through a trap door which had a guard round it to prevent customers falling down the hole." *Tommy White*

"F.W. Higgins was the name of another sweet shop, just about at 5 Swan Street. He struck me as odd and we used to go around mimicking him as kids do. He seemed quite a gentle chap and used to do fabulous jelly babies in there, they were soft in powder, not those hard Bassett things. And he had a chewing gum machine outside, with every fourth turn it *coughed up an extra one*." *Don Hughes*

"When the boys were young - they're in their 40s now - I would do all my shopping around Isleworth, John Quality, Harry Agate, greengrocers, Goddard, shoe repairers and a shoe shop, Betty Bigwood. Now it's all supermarkets." *Josie Best*

"There were lots of different greengrocers and Platt's International Stores. I remember that I used to come down to South Street to get shoes for the boy for school. It's all very different now. Things have changed. We could do with a nice butcher, instead of a shop along there that sells ceiling roses!" *Mary Crickmore*

Mrs. Mary Edith Curtis, shopkeeper, and Mrs. Rosa Abel, grocer, at Nos. 34 and 19 North Street respectively, appear in Kelly's Directory 1937 – early closing day was Wednesday. Jas Pooley, grocer, Worple Road is listed in 1933.

"We used to go to Mrs. Abel's corner shop and Mrs. Curtis' general grocers. We'd collect lemonade bottles from along the river to Richmond and put them in a big sack. They were in short supply. Mrs. Curtis gave us pennies in return but used to get *a bit browned off* when we took in up to a hundred." *Peter Farmer*

"The family shopped at Pooley's in Worple Road. It was a sort of hut or shed almost opposite Napier Road." *Mrs. Wrangles*

"In St. John's Road at the end of the Rec, Mr. & Mrs. Cobb *sold fruit and veg from their front room*. They spent hours sitting outside the front door. There was a shop called Smith's at the end of Grainger Road. I was sent with a note for half an ounce of Nosegay tobacco and two eggs – "make sure they are fresh" I was told. As prices never varied the money was put in the envelope with the note. Imagine the terror I suffered as I carried two eggs home in a paper bag." *Joan Butler*

"In the 1940s we had a radio with an accumulator which had to be taken to be charged at a local hardware store. I had to go down Jolly's Alley and was always told to *"be careful, and not to run"* because it contained acid." *Pam Strickland*

"On the Twickenham Road near Chestnut Grove, where the fish and chip shop is now used to be a greengrocer, they made deliveries. The butcher was next, then a hardware store – open all hours, *smelt of paraffin* but you could get everything there, just a few screws if you wanted them rather than a whole box. There was always an off licence and paper shop, this was privately owned until Forbuoys took it over. At the back of the Post Office at one time was a hairdresser's. An Asian family ran the general grocer shop." *Kit Turner*

"There was a group of shops in Linkfield Road at the junction with Kendall Road. The corner shop was a grocer, next Fred Fielder, greengrocer, also a sweet shop – with lots of jars of sweets lined up

- and a butcher. Very handy just across the road, now they are all houses." *Alma Bignall*

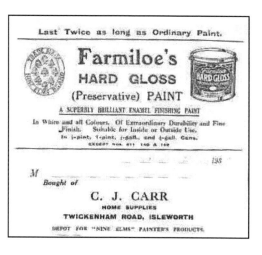

"At Ivybridge, above the Keymarket store was MFI, and along the parade a launderette, Fuller's Off Licence, Coombs the bakers, and a good butcher. An 'Outdoor' shop sold riding gear and catered for hobbies. There was a bookies, hairdresser and an excellent Chinese Restaurant called something like Diners' Cottage, not to mention the Harlequin Pub which had *something of a dark reputation."* Alan Cooke

St. John's Superstore held a Grand Opening attended by the Mayoress of Hounslow on Friday 5th December 1997 at 11 a.m. Special offers included Heinz Baked Beans 420 grms for only 25p, Stella Artois 330 ml bottle 65p. Opening hours 6 a.m. – 10 p.m. seven days a week.

During the 1980s, shoppers began looking elsewhere:
"Went into Brentford, got mum's suspender belts and went in to the bank. Looks as if the Co-op hasn't got much longer to go. They might as well close, they cannot compete with the International." *Mary Jolley's diary, 9 November 1982*

"Went over to Hounslow. The Co-op had their closing down sale. Did OK over there. Got pillowcases and net curtains for back bedroom, 33% off makes a big difference. Had a bit of luck in Marks, bought Alf some blue thermal underpants/vest but was only charged for one pair so saved £3.25, not bad. And what with about £4.00 in the Co-op it was worth the trip." *Mary Jolley's diary, 22nd November 1982*

But many stayed and flourished:
"Mother had the cafe on Twickenham Road 1921 until 1947 then I took over and carried on until 1961 – it was called The Isleworth Dining Rooms." *Rosemary Chatfield*

Most of the shopkeepers have been trading in St. John's Road for many years. Among these is Peter Gohegan who owns Mr. Bun the Baker. Every piece of bread is made fresh on the premises each day. Another is Mike

Roser of Londis. He's the original friendly shopkeeper who knows all his customers and gives them personal care and attention. J. Golding Newsagent has been resident for nearly a decade. Since the local wool shop closed, Jasim's Pharmacy has a wide range of wool and accessories amongst other unusual items from which to choose. Hounslow Recorder, 28th November 1997

"Mollie Bradley married Harry, brother of Mr. Lillyman, the butcher. There's no-one of the family in the business now but the London Road shop still carries the name." *Grace Cousins*

75 year old Norman Taylor and his wife Grace will be jetting off by Concorde in May on a holiday won in a competition organised by security lock company Chubb. Established in 1885, Norman's hardware store, T. Taylor and Sons in South Street had been supplying locks longer than any other firm in the country. Hounslow Informer, February 1994

F. Fenn & Son, jewellers and watchmakers, was established 1910 in the London Road. The 1926 telephone directory lists their number as HOUNSLOW 1890 - now it is 020 8560 1890.

The Upper Square in the early 1900's

A pre 1900 grocery discount token later used by Parker's Stores

chapter two
Getting About

Goat & Trap
Dad once bought a goat which was kept in the garden. His idea was it would take the children for rides in a little trap. He also bought the trap. *Unfortunately, the goat was a male* and impossible to train. We had many a laugh trying to get it to do what we wanted."
Frank Winterborne

Horse
"The brewery horses were always, to my mind, such a lovely sight. Children would take a barrow and gather up, from the brewery yards, the *free manure for their dads' gardens.*" *Mrs. E.Woodland*

"Mann's were the market garden proprietors in Worton Road. I remember the horse and carts loaded with baskets. We used to collect the horse droppings; *it made good fertiliser* and dad was a keen gardener." *Bert Kendall*

Bicycle
"In South Street was Mr. Hill's cycle shop where you could *hire a bicycle for a few pence* and take a happy ride out with no buses or cars to trouble you as there are now – or not many anyway, as everything on the roads was horse driven." *Mrs. E.Woodward*

"The 'boy' delivered our groceries which were loaded into a large basket balanced on the front of his bicycle." *Grace Cousins*

"Initially I travelled by 37 bus, on my own, but later cycled to the Town School, not only to and from it, but home to dinner and back." *Leslie Wrangles*

"I cycled back and forth to school, four and a half miles. Later, when I worked at West Middlesex Hospital, transport from Cranford was two buses and a walk so I either cycled or motor cycled." *Lorna Newman*

"We must have wasted hours travelling between the different school buildings, you were *not allowed to get a bus* and those who owned a bicycle were much envied." *Pauline Betts*

Fire Engine

"The foundry, run by Mr. Winterborne, was home to the fire escape ladders. These came to fires by horse and cart some time after the early fire engine which was housed in the small fire station next to the War Memorial. Before a motor fire engine was acquired, the building housed an antiquated steam vehicle with a big brass chimney in the middle, two large wooden wheels at the back and two small ones at the front. It did, I believe, a maximum of 40 m.p.h. The driver for years *was a portly gentleman* called Mr. Hubbard whose stomach just managed to get behind the steering wheel." *Arthur Wenden*

Tram

"A great adventure of school was the four mile journey to Gumley on a tram. This involved hailing it from the kerb and then negotiating cars and horses and carts to the middle of the High Road, climbing up three steep steps and perching on seats, with feet dangling. The thrill of *lurching along with brakes screeching* and wheels rattling in the tramlines was exciting." *Cecilia Whelan*

All Kind of Buses

"The first buses to run from Isleworth were white steam ones with open tops and aprons to *cover you up a bit when it rained*. The electric trams with overhead wires also ran along Twickenham Road to Hampton and Hammersmith." *Mrs. E. Woodland*

"The camber of South Street was very steep, if the 37 bus came round the corner from Twickenham Road too close to the curb *its top deck would hit the balcony* of Balch's butcher shop." *Arthur Wenden*

"Around 1935 the London Road tram depot was enlarged to take trolley buses. The trolley buses used to be lined up outside our house - we would go out and *ding the bells*." *John Benn*

"One away football match we played was at West Hounslow. At Hounslow Bus Garage I discovered there was a bus strike so walked to Hounslow West, played the match and walked back to Isleworth. Mr. Brown, the Headmaster, got to hear about it and had me up on the stage at assembly and said nice things about me. *I was so embarrassed*." *Leslie Lees*

"Only the 37 bus and trolley bus served Isleworth at that time. The 37 was always crowded despite being double deckers with a 15 minute leeway and *it had to make a small detour* as it could not get under the railway bridge in St. John's Road." *Lorna Newman*

A delivery van outside Hounslow Model Laundry London Road, Isleworth

"Most people travelled by public transport, walked, or rode bicycles. Trolley buses were used, these ran on electricity supplied by overhead wires. Sometimes the arms would come off the wires and the conductor would *have to get a long pole out* from underneath the floor of the bus to link them back again. They accelerated very quickly and smoothly and I often felt sick, especially when I travelled to Hammersmith." *Pam Strickland*

"One of my duties as a teacher at the Blue School involved escorting children to the 37 bus stop after school and seeing them on board." *Pauline Betts*

"On 8th May 1962 I got off at Busch Corner the junction with route 657 which I'd selected for *my last ever ride* on a London trolley bus system. I walked the couple of miles to its Hounslow terminus, past the Isleworth

Railway Station.—South Western, Henry Baker, station master

Conveyance.—Electric tram-cars pass through every few minutes from Hammersmith & Shepherd's Bush to Twickenham & Hampton Court
Motor omnibuses from Herne Hill, via Brixton, Clapham Junction, Putney, Richmond & Twickenham, every 6 or 7 minutes
Ferry for passengers from Church street to Richmond ; Arthur Simmonds, ferryman

BUS SERVICES.

Route 27.—Hounslow Garage to Twickenham, Richmond, Hammersmith and Highgate.
    37.} Hounslow Heath to Isleworth, St. Margaret's, Richmond, Wandsworth, Clapham Common and
    201.}   Peckham.
    81.—Hounslow Garage to Windsor Castle.
    65.—Hounslow to Harlington and Hayes.
    116.—Hounslow to Ascot. (Sundays and Public Holidays).
    116a.—Hounslow to Staines Bridge.
    116b.—Hounslow to Virginia Water.
    117.—Hounslow to Windsor.
    120a.—Hounslow Heath to Southall via The " Bell," Heston Church and Norwood Green.
London to Bristol Grey Coaches pass through Hounslow twice daily.

RAILWAY SERVICES.

District Railway.

		Hounslow West.	Hounslow Central.	Hounslow East.	Osterley.
First train	Week-days	5.16 a.m.	5.18 a.m.	5.20 a.m.	5.22 a.m.
	Sundays	7.46 a.m.	7.50 a.m.	7.52 a.m.	7.54 a.m.
Last train	Week-days	11.37 p.m.	11.39 p.m.	11.41 p.m.	11.43 p.m.
for City	Sundays	10.47 p.m.	10.49 p.m.	10.51 p.m.	10.53 p.m.
Last train not	Week-days	12.15 p.m.	12.17 p.m.	12.19 p.m.	12.21 p.m.
beyond Acton	Sundays	11.50 p.m.	11.52 p.m.	11.54 p.m.	11.47 p.m.
Last train Acton to Hounslow. Week-days 1.7 a.m., Sundays 12.40 p.m.					

Southern Railway.

Hounslow to Waterloo.—First train 5.9 a.m. Half-hourly service. with intermediate trains during morning and
evening "rush" hours. Last train 11.9 p.m.
Sundays.—First train 8 a.m. Last train 1¼ p.m.
Hounslow to Twickenham.—First train 6.24 a.m. Half-hourly service. Last train 10.54 p.m.
Sundays.—First train 8.50 a.m. Last train 10.30 p.m.
Waterloo to Hounslow.—First train 5.49 a.m. Half-hourly service with intermediate trains during morning and
evening "rush" hours. Last train 11.49 p.m.
Sundays.—First train 7.45 p.m. Last train 11.15 p.m.

TRAM SERVICES.

		Week-days,		Sundays.	
		First car.	Last car.	First car.	Last car.
Hounslow and		4.46 a.m.	11.18 p.m.	8.18 a.m.	11.18 p.m.
Shepherd's Bush		5.30 a.m.	11.35 p.m.	9.0 a.m.	11.35 p.m.
	Interval	8 minutes.		6 minutes.	
Cars from Hammersmith for					
Twickenham, Hampton Court					
and Kingston pass through					
Isleworth	Interval	6 minutes.		5 minutes	

depot, which housed just one route the 657. Then I boarded for my final ride – EXVI04 I have the ticket still." *David Gourley*

"Went to the International today to get the shopping. Of course I had too much as usual, makes it a struggle to get on the bus – mind you it's easier on a Thursday, not so crowded. I suppose, now I have a free bus pass, I could go to the International twice a week." *Mary Jolley's diary, 28 October 1982*

"We knew the tram and bus conductors by name. There were some great comedians, real characters. They enjoyed their jobs; wore collars and ties and looked smart. We would go regularly to Acton - the conductor knew I could sing and would say, "*give us a song*" – I got pennies for doing it." *Ray Farnden*

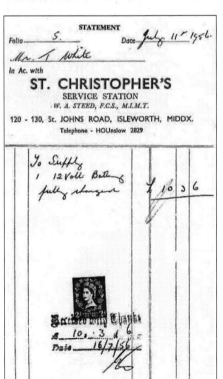

STATEMENT

Folio _____ S.

Date _July. 11th 1956._

Mr. T. White

In Ac. with

ST. CHRISTOPHER'S
SERVICE STATION
. W. A. STEED, F.C.S., M.I.M.T.
120 - 130, St. JOHNS ROAD, ISLEWORTH, MIDDX.
Telephone - HOUnslow 2829

To Supply
1 12 Volt Battery
fully charged   £10. 3. 6

Received with Thanks

£ 10. 3. 6
Date 16/7/56

Hitching a Ride

"Going home from school via Wood Lane the Watney Brewery drays and those of Beatties the coal merchant used to provide our gang with a 'lift' as we hung on the chains conveniently hung down the back. Motor driven trucks, including Foden steam trucks, provided the same facility. But the greater speed increased the danger of being carried *miles past home* and we gambled on the hope that the Southern Railway level crossing was closed or the lights at the Great West Road at 'red' so we could thankfully drop off." *Brian Cullum*

Wheelchair

"Early expeditions were highly experimental and Church Street, where we lived, is still far from ideal for any sort of wheelchair. On one "walk" Margaret actually *tipped out of her chair* on the bridge over the Duke of Northumberland's river. There was no way I could get her back unaided. Without hesitation, two passing workmen jovially hoisted Margaret up and back again as if it were all part of their day's work." *John Ray*

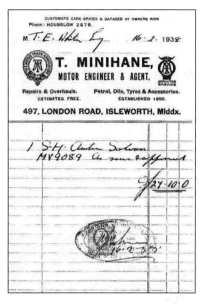

The Railway

"One way home was along the trolley bus route to Busch Corner, past the car wrecking yard, and up Quaker Lane. *We could have a swing* on the apparatus in the new recreation ground. If we could hear it coming, we'd rush up the steps of the new footbridge over the railway and wait for the steam train to engulf us in soot and smoke." *Brian Cullum*

Things Can Only Get Better – it's been dubbed one of the worst stations in London. Isleworth station is falling to bits. But at last something IS being done. The Informer, March 1995

Car

"There were only two car owners in South Street when I was a child in the 1920s, two of the shopkeepers." *Arthur Wenden*

"Traffic on our journey to school was very light, except maybe during Ascot Week, as the Great West Road was not yet opened. And there was *always a friendly policeman* to see us safely over the main road." *Grace Cousins*

"Petrol was on ration but several of our school mistresses at Gumley were given sufficient allowances, as it was too difficult for them to get to school by bus." *Lorna Newman*

"My first car was a Wolesey Hornet – I would use it to

make deliveries. It was much quieter in the 1940s, with only a few cars. I still drive, keep my car in a garage at the back of Swann Court." *Charlie Self*

"The Lobjoits were nearby market gardeners, you saw their many lorries on the road loaded with round baskets holding the fruit." *Bert Kendall*

Treble Green Shield stamps on offer c.1970 at St. Christopher's garage

"When I took over the St. Christopher's garage business in 1965 customers could get four gallons of petrol *and some change from £1*. Petrol was delivered 4,100 gallons at a time and we sold 17,000 gallons each month. Green Shield stamps ate into the profit but were for a time a fashionable necessity. Customers saved them to get free gifts from the suppliers of the stamps." *Michael Becker*

"I took my first driving lesson in the February and passed my test in September – I was age 42 – and very proud of myself." *Ann Cooke*

A child was nearly knocked down outside school this week due to the number of parked cars on the zigzag lines – this in spite of numerous reminders in newsletters and notices placed on windscreens. Please, for everyone's sake DO NOT PARK ON THE ZIGZAG LINES (Worple Primary School News, Issue 101, November 2001)

Walking
"We've never had a car. From Harewood Road I walked to St. John's Road to work, my husband to Mogden. And, of course, the boys walked to school." *Margaret Kendall*

"My mum never had any money so we used to walk everywhere. We'd walk to Heston where my dad was buried – think nothing then of walking three or four miles and the same coming back. People just didn't have cars then." *Lionel Watson*

"From school we went every week to Isleworth baths, about a mile away. We all walked there together and back to school afterwards, even if it was home time

when we arrived back." *Pam Strickland*

"There was a bus strike so I walked from Richmond to work at Fluidrive in Worton Road, taking a short cut down Queen's Terrace and Brantwood Avenue. When I saw the houses in Brantwood the dream of owning one was way off. Later, out of the blue, a similar house in Worple Road came up – *just what we wanted*, with a garage and our own drive. We purchased it 20th October 1956 and I've been there ever since." *Joan Baxter*

Around 1972 the 'lollipop' man in South Street retired. There was a long gap and no replacement was allocated, so Beryl Rowland, concerned at seeing the children risk their lives crossing the road, decided she would do the job unofficially. All the mothers took turns to hold up the traffic, using a *home-made 'lollipop' sign*. Eventually a new man, Pop Hillier, appeared on the scene and then did the job for many years." *Shirley Bascran*

"Marion Chapman has been 'lollipop' lady since 1978 and there have been no accidents in that time. A few years' ago, when they put the pedestrian crossing in along South Street, there was a danger of the job being lost. Fortunately this did not happen." *Pam Booth*

D.L.11 No. 11/ 2023102
GREATER LONDON COUNCIL
ROAD TRAFFIC ACT 1960
PROVISIONAL DRIVING LICENCE
Fee of 10/- received

Civic duty - Rosemary Coomber, Kate Williamson and Sandy Rahman re-plant the horse trough in Upper Square

Branch Line - train topiary at Woodland Gardens

In the frame - members of the St. Johns Residents Association enjoy a guided tour of Old Isleworth in 1995

*Church Street residents raising money
for Comic Relief in 1988*

chapter three
Village Life

**The bees swarmed at noon and were
hived after school. Every child in
each department was taken into the orchard to see the swarm while it hung on
a plum tree.** Isleworth Town Boys School log, 1911

"Living in Isleworth there were always different smells – from Pears Soap Works, the
Brewery and (still) Mogden." *Leslie Wrangles*

"The old Liberal Party was in decline and it was mostly Labour v Conservative. One
of the amusing sidelines of this concerned a Mr. Fielder and his mother. He was
originally a fiery orator and leader of the local Labour Party, who later mellowed into
a well respected Councillor. His mother was a staunch Conservative. When our local
M.P. Joyson Hicks (who was Home Secretary for years) held an election meeting at
the Public Hall you would see Mrs. Fielder patting him on the back as he left, while
her son stood on the opposite pavement *shouting near obscenities* at him."
Arthur Wenden

"In the 1920s we lived in a small bungalow. It was cold in winter, the only fireplace
was in the living room, the three bedrooms were candle lit but we did have an indoor
lavatory." *Ray Farnden*

"We were encouraged to save our pennies and once a week could buy National
Savings stamps at 6d each. I can still see those stamps, which we stuck on a card
until we had saved 16 shillings, which would buy a certificate. They were *red with
a white swastika* on them – a sign of good fortune until Mr. Hitler used it for
the Nazis! Certificates could be exchanged for cash at the Post Office at any time or
held on to as an investment." *Grace Cousins*

"Mrs. Minnie Whenman used to deliver the babies. My mother had eight and she
delivered six of us. She lived at the top end of Linkfield Road. It was a different world
– we used to go to Bluebell Woods near the Hare and Hounds, Osterley. We'd have
skipping in the street with the rope right across the road; seasons came round,

first spinning tops, then marbles and cigarette cards." *Josie Best*

"A 'convenience' missing in most local households was a bathroom, so the slipper baths attached to the small swimming pool at the rear of the Public Hall was a great boon. I think it cost 3d." *Arthur Wenden*

"*The first Dr. Who* lived in Church Street opposite the London Apprentice. They'd play cricket at the back. He would call the kids in to help collect up the balls. Margaret Rutherford lived nearly next door and Joan Hickson lived down there at one time. They were all very friendly, would talk to you, not snobbish at all." *Theresa Turner*

"Dr. Waterston lived in one of the houses opposite the London Apprentice and I remember he operated on Prince Charles when he had appendicitis." *Alice Phipps*

"I lived in May Villa, Byfield Road and us local kids used to enjoy the excitement of scrumping apples from the grounds of Bears Honey. When our road was going to be re-surfaced a large pile of lime chippings was delivered – we threw a lot over the walls attempting to knock down apples for us to collect later. Suddenly the gate in the wall opened; the owner came out and told us to pick up all the chippings, *offering us 2d each*. We did, and he paid up!" *Ken Norman*

"My grandmother was from the area, lived in Linkfield Road for a while. I have pretty long roots here and the next generation seem to be staying." *Ian Macklearn*

"In Mogden Lane was Mann's orchard – we used to go scrumping but never got caught. *We were too fast* for that." *Terry Percival*

"We had no electricity until 1952, no bathroom till 1964. A tin bath was put on the kitchen floor, filled with hot water from a copper - for a time the water was heated by a coal fire. One room, the living room, was heated by an open fire, and only one of the three bedrooms had a gas light. *We had an outside toilet* and chamber

pots were very much used. The bedrooms were freezing in winter with ice on the inside of the windows." *Pam Strickland*

"Mr. Titchmarsh the village bobby lived in North Street. When the children were naughty, he'd say, *"I'll tell your mother"*. Taylor's Wharfage owned houses in Church Street including at one time number 38 where we lived. Curtis & Harvey owned houses there too. Our rent was 10s a week." *Theresa Turner*

"In the dream time of childhood, I remember blackthorn blossom, making sandwiches of the leaves, apples picked and eaten straight from our trees in the garden, no chemical insecticides then. We went bird nesting and fishing for newts. Were scrubbed behind the ears with *Family Health Soap* and sent to bed with Fry's Cocoa. We listened to Toytown on the radio's Children's Hour - a full 60 minutes - and joined the Ovalteenies. We were in the Cubs and the church choir." *Brian Cullum*

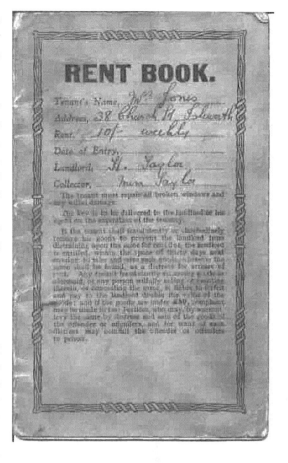

"Scrumping was a good activity in the autumn, the more exotic fruit you could get the more you went up in the *peer pressure group line!* We used to go to what was called Father's Gardens at the rear of the Catholic Father's house. He had a few trees there. There was a peach tree in Silverhall Street, it meant walking along the back walls to get the fruit. The best thing I remember was stealing strawberries out of an allotment up past Ivy Bridge." *Don Hughes*

"The first ring-necked parakeets I ever saw were in 1952. I saw them down the ferry not far from Syon Park. Magpie sized birds, grass green with *long pointy tails*, swift flight and an urgent cry of Phwee! Phwee!" *Lionel Watson*

First World War veterans gather in Church Street

Watney's Isleworth Brewery was almost directly opposite, giving the site a distinctive and sometimes confusing character. School was often conducted to the intoxicating smell of boiling beer, especially on Tuesdays. Pears' soap factory was also within inhaling distance, if winds were northerly. A History of Isleworth Grammar School

Lee's Greengrocers
Upper Square

"My wife worked for Lee's, greengrocers. Mrs. Lee let us live at the shop when we had nowhere to go. It was in poor condition and we worked on it for years. Her son Gordon was a great help. When we took the walls down we found them *fixed to trees*. The bedroom's still wattle and daub. It dates from c1690. Mrs. Lee only charged a very small rent. When she died we found she'd left our part of it for us to live in rent free for the rest of our lives, and no-one could live next door that we did not approve of." *Ray Farnden*

"The Carers' Group used to meet in the library. Just some 10 or so of us. Sandy Rahman was very good, she did all the clerical work and organising. We had speakers sometimes, ranging from the Heritage Guides, to information about nursing homes." *Kit Turner*

22

Church Street cottages

When I was a lad I'd talk to a neighbour, Les Mortimer, about the aeroplanes – I rather liked the sound of piston engines, found them comforting. He suggested, if I listened carefully early morning, I would hear the mail plane come in from France. I did - it was a Heinkel *– an ex-German bomber* was being used to fly our mail!" *Geoffrey Drew*

"On Sunday evening dad used to 'groom' his bowler hat and he and mum walked us through the Woodlands to Riverside Walk, then round Mogden Sewage works. In those days it was like the country – no smells then." *Joan Butler*

"Riverside Walk was originally a cul-de-sac and its character very different from now. The only commercial vehicles seen were those delivering to houses. Car ownership of residents was tiny compared with today. The land to the east of the river was still under cultivation and the copse along the east bank much denser, with displays of guelder roses and lilacs in the spring. There were also some mature ash trees and of course plenty of willows. It was quite reasonable of the developer to install seats and a small summer house to adorn this peaceful scene. He could hardly have anticipated the growth of aviation, and the flight paths to Heathrow!" *Tom Walters*

"We called the summer house in Riverside Walk, Soloman's Temple – a Mr. Soloman who lived near by looked after it.

The boys would congregate on one side, girls the other, and we'd *shout to each other* over the top." *Pauline Hooper*

What has 18 streets, 1,000 households, 59 shops, three pubs and a park? Answer: St. John's Residents Association which covers the area bounded by London Road, Twickenham Road, Linkfield and St. John's Roads. Its aim is to protect and enhance the environment of that area. St. John's Residents Association Newsletter, October 1991

"The best part of living locally in the old days - the natural beauty and simplicity of the district, a garden with the river. The worst - a lot of poverty and so much drunkenness and fighting when I was a child. My favourite walk when we were courting was right through what is now Worple Avenue, out to Twickenham Road, which was then more an avenue of huge trees with their roots spread out all over the pavements. Sweet Briar Alley out to Mogden Lane was so pretty too." *Mrs. E. Woodland*

"The side of the Twickenham Road opposite the hospital did not have any houses. There were bushes and behind these, one half had rhubarb growing and the other was covered in rotting vegetables. Where the telephone exchange now is was a *pear orchard*. There were two alleyways between the Twickenham Road and London Road, one coming out at the Rising Sun and the other the Rose and Crown; also a long alley between the hospital and cemetery." *Mary Huxley*

"I was born in Isleworth, the family's been here for five generations both halves of the family, the Dickers and the Hicks. My grandparents lived at 16 Byfield Road. I remember everything was so dark and gloomy. Grandfather, Nipper Hicks, had this lovely box with all the brushes and grooming stuff for the horse. He made the box himself. He was a bit of an amateur cabinet maker, he had all these lathes and stuff *in the shed* at the bottom of his garden." *Rob Dickers*

"We lived in Mandeville Road. Originally there was a house there called Mandeville House and then they built 36 houses and a bungalow. We were the last house in the row but the marvellous thing about it was the big house at the end had a huge orchard surrounded by a wall. So all the gardens were really orchards and everybody that moved in had *loads of fruit*. We had about five fruit trees when my parents moved in around 1939." *Joan 'Molly' Brown*

"My brother and I were Scouts. We used to go down to Uncle Mac who ran the

The family of Charles Phipps - flour miller of Church Street

London Apprentice. There'd always be something to do like chopping wood to get money for the Bob A Job Week." *Keith Knight*

"As a widow moving here in 1985, I felt it was a bonus living on the Twickenham Road - three doors away was the Doctors' surgery, just up the road West Middlesex Hospital and opposite, Paine's the funeral directors!" *Pam Booth*

"When we first moved to Arnold Crescent it was much like living in the countryside with fields and orchards. *We still have rhubarb* growing in our garden - it was well established when we came." *Barbara Friend*

"There used to be some allotments in the Borough Road College grounds where it bordered the Great West Road and also in Wood Lane North. We benefited as a family from dad's hard work there, as well as in our own garden, with home grown vegetables." *Iris Evans*

"I was looking for a two bedroom cottage and made an appointment to view. By coincidence, my mother rang me to say she had found a promising property – it

Mogden House Nursery
Established over Half a Century

WHOLESALE & RETAIL
NURSERYMEN

•

Bedding Plants of every
description
Shrubs, etc. Cut Flowers

FRESH PICKED TOMATOES

Chrysanthemum Cuttings
INSPECTION INVITED

•

MOGDEN HOUSE
TWICKENHAM ROAD, ISLEWORTH, MIDDX.

was the same one! I liked it first off, and also the fact that all the cottages in Algar Road are different. Then I walked down to the river and church where there was a sailing dingy on the slipway. It all looked so nice I knew it was the place for me."
Carolyne Vines

"The family lived in Worton Road from the time I was two – there were orchards behind the house. The trees came up to our back garden, mainly apples and pears not much soft fruit around there. I was always *woken by bird songs* – there were many woodpeckers in those days." *Bert Kendall*

"I shall never forget Isleworth and, who knows, I may get back one day. We made a mistake by leaving. Now we have a tiny cottage near Bath which will never be home to me although the countryside is beautiful. But *give me the jumbo jets* and the sweet aroma of Mogden as it was years ago."
Gladys Willsher

Mogden - home for aromas

"We were newcomers in the 1980s. Gradually we got to know and enjoy most of what Isleworth offered in way of lifestyle – the library and swimming pool, the extraordinarily sociable Post Office, All Saints with its unlikely modern interior. But, when Margaret became a wheelchair user, it would be difficult to imagine a less suitable house. Margaret could just about get through the garage, cross the back garden and use one ground floor room. *A keen Italian* tried out a novel stair hopping wheelchair that could tackle virtually anything – even he had to admit defeat. It says a lot for the place that we tried all sort of ideas to enable us to remain." *John Ray*

chapter four
Time Gentlemen Please!

While some 18 public houses remain, several have pulled their last pint. The King's Arms was a recent casualty, joining The Labouring Boys, Waterman's Arms, Duke of Cornwall and Northumberland Arms, names that reflect the area's history.

"One likeable, gregarious, generous publican was also a bit of a wheeler-dealer. A brewery held a competition in which the pub that sold the most of its own brand lager in the south of England would be the winner. This enterprising man attached barrels of the lager to all his lager pumps. *Unsuspecting customers* drank it without noticing - and he won a holiday on the continent!" *Paul Turner*

The Standard, South Street
"The pubs have not altered much, only in size. One outstanding one was The Standard where you would so often see and hear *a man called Cecil* playing a whistle for a living. This was opposite a square of cottages called Stafford Alley." *Mrs. E. Woodland*

The Castle, Upper Square
"Mr. Lee, greengrocer, used to keep the coal he sold in the Castle Yard before the pub was re-built. There were eight houses at the side. One room up, one room down with a hall - the toilets were across the yard, *also the wash house*." *Theresa Turner*

The London Apprentice, Church Street
"My godfather was landlord. There was a pinball machine which cost, I think, one old penny. We would always go and play on it upstairs in the function room where the dining room is now. Downstairs was a children's room - *kids weren't allowed* in the public or saloon bars

The Duke of Northumberland PH

but the thing I will always remember was the sound of dominoes being played." *Keith Knight*

Northumberland Arms, (later called Duke of Northumberland and Inn on the Square) Lower Square
"You couldn't get in the door of the Northumberland Arms on Sunday nights it was so packed. We were called The Rhythm Band, and people joined in the singing. Jack Cannon was the proprietor, an ex-sailor with one leg. Ran it for years. Had a Mynah bird on the counter. It was a popular ritual to say to it, "where's Jack"? and it said back *"down the cellar with a blonde".* *Ray Farnden*

The Rythm Band: Les Donald (drums), Eddie Bowry (bass), Bill Bowry (piano) & Ray Farnden (guitar)

The Woodlands, Woodlands Road
"We often went in there before family or friends' weddings at the nearby church – it was called the Railway Tavern at that time." *Kit Turner*

King's Arms, South Street
There was rock music on Sunday mornings. I went in unawares once and thought it a bit noisy but bought my pint, then found the bass was so loud *the floor was moving* and I was gliding along it." *Alan Cooke*

The Victoria, Worple Road
"In the early 80s, Dave and Edna's time, it was very much a village pub." *Alan Cooke*

28

Red Lion, Linkfield Road
"We spent many happy hours there. Danny played the piano and everyone joined in singing along with country and western style songs." *Kit Turner*

Jolly Gardeners (now Triple Crown) Twickenham Road
"I lived in Chestnut Grove, which is at the end of the row of shops, from the age of one until I got married. The Jolly Gardeners pub is where my husband and I held our wedding reception in August 1966." *Mary Smith*

"We had our wedding reception in the function room. Later a group of us fell into meeting there a couple of evenings a week after our various work shifts ended. One was a detective, another worked for Chubb, others at Heathrow and West Middlesex Hospital; we worked at Ranton in Brentford. Some 12-14 in all, we called it the Happy Hour, *happy to be off work*. It was a convivial place, the only pub where, as a woman, I felt comfortable to go in on my own. Sunday lunch times were enjoyable. It was well run." *Ann Cooke*

We can look forward to a return to traditional values at The Triple Crown, following their fantastic refurbishment. Previously the Jolly Gardeners, there has been a high concentration on quality, service and sensible pricing.
Hounslow Informer, 10 May 2002

The Rythm Band entertaining at the Jolly Gardeners

Chequers, Twickenham Road
"The food was home made when Pat and Lucy O'Hara ran it. It was always busy, used a lot by the doctors and nurses from West Middlesex. *They often held parties* in the function room at the back. It's all open plan now." *Sarah Douglas*

29

The Swan, Corner North and Swan Street

"I cook my own mid-day meal, except at weekends when I go to Greedies, South Street. When they were closed for 10 days around Christmas I went to The Swan. They've recently had a change of management and started doing meals again." *Charlie Self*

The George, Twickenham Road

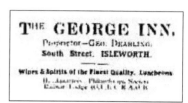

"My grandfather, who worked as a drayman, also had a part time job as a barman. We used to go to this sort of private back room when we were kids and he'd supply us with lemonade." *Rob Dickers*

THE GEORGE INN,
Proprietor—Geo. Dearling,
South Street. ISLEWORTH.

Wines & Spirits of the Finest Quality. Luncheons

And other Spirits....

"The London Apprentice had a ghostly sailor in an upstairs room."

"We were told at school that Lady Jane Grey's ghost walked on the foreshore opposite the eyot on moonlight nights. She'd had her head cut off and came back to Isleworth to make a fuss. The eyot itself, a great tangle of trees, had a hermit as ghost."

"Two much more substantial ghosts - the first was Vincent Van Gogh, seen only once in sunlight, standing opposite The Swan. That's where Isleworth Green is now, but c1950 it was a derelict flattened bomb site."

"The other ghost was *a man of the road*. There he was one evening. I've long since forgotten his clothes but they were unkempt. Red hair and his beard the same. Quite young looking still and grinning at me." *Lionel Watson*

The Northumberland Arms, converted in the 1980's to offices - now renamed "Waverley House"

The Old Castle Inn - a lino cut by C. Burgess 4A Smallberry Green School - 1949

Chapter Five
Men of the Road

ISLEWORTH CASUAL WARDS—wood-chopping sheds

In the 19th century homeless men 'on tramp' could obtain food and shelter for one night at casual wards located throughout the country. By the end of the 1930s there were only two in Middlesex, one at Edmonton the other Isleworth.

A 50 year old man was sent to prison for seven days with hard labour for neglecting to perform his allotted tasks while a casual pauper at Isleworth Workhouse. He had been told by the Labour Master to break ten hundredweight of stone but had told him to "Boil 'em". *Press cutting, February 1900*

"My uncle used to pick hops in Kent. When he returned he would not stay with any of his relations but insisted he enjoyed *staying at the Workhouse*. Dundee House in Mill Plat was used for children from the Workhouse, all the children went out for walks holding hands." *Theresa Turner*

"Where the houses are in Amhurst Gardens was an old alley with market gardens both sides, the old tramps, mostly men and very dirty, used to *sleep in the hedges*. Children were afraid to go down there. Where the West Middlesex Hospital car park is used to be a high wall with a small gate where tramps queued up to go in for a night's sleep and a meal." *Elsie Burnell*

"We walked to and from Spring Grove Junior twice a day, as we came home to a mid-day meal. Morning school finished at 12.00 and we had to be back by 2 p.m., then lessons continued till 4 p.m. This meant we were often walking home at dusk in winter but no-one ever seemed to come to any harm. We did, however, hurry past the part of the London Road where the Odeon cinema was later built. In the 1920s that piece of land was a little spinney and *quite dark and spooky* so we never dawdled there. Year in, year out, there were always tramps trudging along to the Workhouse adjoining the West Middlesex Hospital, or infirmary as it was generally called. They could get a meal and bed for the night." *Grace Cousins*

31

"The jam jar man gave you a windmill in exchange for a jam jar. Another gave you a ride on a roundabout pulled around the streets by a horse. Men would walk in the centre of the road singing, or push a *pram with a wind up gramophone* in it. You would give them a penny or half penny."

"On Sundays the winkle man and muffin man would come round the streets. Pip used to sell vegetables cheap which he bought from Brentford market, because the goods were on the verge of going rotten. Women buying peas from him would lift their aprons and he would shoot them into it. He was very honest and someone convinced him to open a bank account. Eventually the bank manager called him in and told him "you're overdrawn by £17" and Pip got his cheque book out to write a cheque for that amount." *Leslie Lees*

"One attraction for my halfpenny was Wall's *Stop Me and Buy One* ice cream tricycle that used to station itself outside the Town School. The man sold triangular iced fruit flavoured sticks in cardboard sleeves." *Brian Cullum*

Pears' Soap

"Two years ago I used your soap, since when I have used no other"
Punch April 1884

A cartoon used by Pears Soap to become one of the earliest examples of humour in advertising. The joke is based on a testimonial from actress Lillie Langtry in a similar fashion

"A local character was Titch Pearson, a totter who toured the streets with his coster barrow all week, then sold what he could on Saturdays in the car park of the King's Arms." *Ken Norman*

"When I was at Gumley House School, tramps used to come to the door at all times and were given tea. Halfway down Linkfield Road was Pelham's Woodyard. They were show people and in the winter lived there and *brought logs round* on their van to sell." *Joan Butler*

*The marriage at St. Bridget's of
Edith 'Sadie' Sanders to Pat Kearns - 1937*

chapter six
Get Me to the Church

The Congregational
"One of dad's jobs was to stoke the boiler in the cellar. If he thought the sermons were going on too long he would go down to put some more fuel on and make a lot of noise doing so, *much to the amusement* of the congregation." *Frank Winterborne*

All Souls
"At weekends, we went to Sunday School in the mornings at All Souls. We often went again in the evenings, sometimes Dad and Grandma would come too, either All Souls or to St. John's." *Laura Hubbard*

"We went to services three times on a Sunday. I sang in the choir and acted as server. Was also a member of the Church Lads' Brigade from the age of seven until I married." *Leslie Wrangles*

St. John the Baptist
We went quite a lot – I remember going in a pushchair, a canvas pushchair made of carpeting and *I always fell asleep.*" *Laura Hubbard*

"As a Cub, and then Scout – 1st Isleworth – you had to attend Church Parade or were frowned upon, although we went to church every week as a family anyway. Father and mother did a lot of fund raising for the Scouts and a Mr. Lewis ran bingo at the Public Hall. Eventually, enough money was raised to build a Scout Headquarters. *An old war time hut* was bought and re-built on land at the Town School near Amhurst Gardens; it was also let out for weddings and the like, but one night, some years later, it burnt down." *Keith Knight*

All Saints Parish Church
"My son woke me and said "Mummy, it's raining" but when I looked out of the window I saw a glow and said "No it's not raining, it's a fire". It was the old Parish Church.

Words could not express my feelings as I was married from that church and my son was christened there." *Laura Hubbard*

"Our dear church burnt down, thanks to two boys scattering matches. Two Wrens who were boarded with us alerted us to the fire and I well remember standing outside my front door and experiencing extreme heat from the blaze." *Mary Price*

"On Ascension Day and Ash Wednesday we Green School pupils would walk down for a service. Sadly, the church was destroyed by vandals in 1943 but we continued to go there, after temporary repairs." *Pauline Betts*

"I've wandered around the churchyard many a time, noticed how, with the Park Road cemetery opening, the dates on the stones fade out at the 20th century. Burials from Saxon times, via the plague pit, to a lady in 1941. How ever, I used to think, did one smallish place *take so many people?*" *Lionel Watson*

"When I belonged to the Scouts Mr. Dicky White was Scoutmaster, assisted by the Rev. Dr. Rowton and Mr. Somerfield the curate. Activities were held in St. John's Rec, the church hall in South Street and a little room in Hartland Road." *John Beal*

"A young Wesleyan missionary came to Isleworth. He worked very hard. My mother joined his meetings so I attended his services. He took my wedding service at All Saints – we had by that time joined up there. He was Rev. Marsh Rapson." *Mrs. E. Woodland*

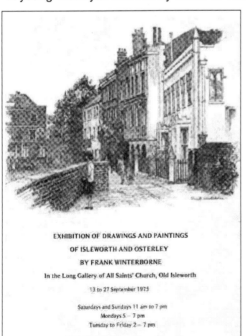

EXHIBITION OF DRAWINGS AND PAINTINGS
OF ISLEWORTH AND OSTERLEY
BY FRANK WINTERBORNE
In the Long Gallery of All Saints' Church, Old Isleworth
13 to 27 September 1975
Saturdays and Sundays 11 am to 7 pm
Mondays 5 – 7 pm
Tuesday to Friday 2 – 7 pm
ADMISSION FREE

"Our elder daughter had a marriage blessing service at the church – an occasion for which my wife, Margaret, consulted not only the vicar's diary *but the tide table* to check that the mud would be hidden beneath a suitably high tide." *John Ray*

"Every church bell was to ring in the new millennium but before this a reporter came to get an idea of what went on at practise night. The story went around the world. Harold Rogers, Tower Captain, received telephone calls from overseas at odd hours, and even a letter simply *addressed to Chief Quasimodo*, The Bell Tower, England." *Maureen Carr*

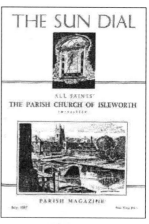

THE SUN DIAL

ALL SAINTS'
THE PARISH CHURCH OF ISLEWORTH

PARISH MAGAZINE

"Sundial, when I first knew it – editor Wally Hughes - was the usual run of Parish magazine. When a new vicar, Derek Hayward, arrived he invested in a printing machine and gathered round him a committee of enthusiasts, most of whom contributed a page each month. A new format was approved and the first issue rolled off the machine July 1966. It grew in popularity, editorship passed to my husband Ken and on its 25th birthday I was promoted to sub-editor. Lynne Reeves, the present editor took over after Ken's death - a difficult job at a difficult time." *Helen Cooper*

St. Bridget's
"My first memory? I think going to church with my father and grandfather. We had a dear dachshund, Kneller – so named because an Army officer from Kneller Hall bred her. She walked very slowly. We went in to church and left Kneller outside tied up. *She objected loudly* to the hymn singing and my father had to go out and speak sharply to her." *Joan Temple*

"Father Green was a lovely man. My mother had come from Ireland, as a maid. She was a good Catholic. We went to church four times on Sunday, 8 a.m., 10.00 or 12.00, then Sunday School, and back in the evening at 6 o'clock. I still get there when I can." *Theresa Turner*

St. Bridget's church fete on a 'Quality Street' theme

Quakers' Meeting House
On Sunday, November 3rd 1935 the Friends of Brentford and Isleworth Meeting House celebrated its 150th anniversary. After the usual morning Meeting for worship, a historical survey of the life of the Meeting was given in the afternoon. About 70 Friends were present and, following tea at The Barn, an inspiring address was given on 'What Have we as a Society to contribute Today?' A Local Quaker History 1785-1985

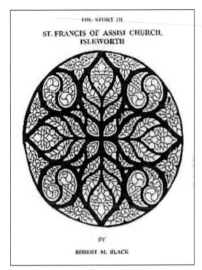

St. Francis of Assisi

"I attended Sunday school regularly from about age six until ten and got very upset once when I was ill and *missed my weekly stamp* for my book – I treasured them. We had extra classes on Saturdays during Lent and received special stamps for this. Each summer we enjoyed a coach trip to Littlehampton, visited the fair and ate candy floss. I also became a Brownie and had to make sure my nails were scrupulously clean and shoes very shiny. We attended Church Parade every month. I loved it all." *Pauline Betts*

The Methodist Church

"I first saw the church in 1944 when I became a student at Borough Road College. For two years a group of students attended there regularly. In 1950 I came to live in Hounslow, was married in the church that year and continued to be active there until 1971 when it closed. The building in which I worshipped dated from 1924. On the site now are four houses approached from Silverhall Street and they are remarkably similar to the church which stood there." *Reg Germany*

Sunday School

"The Harrow family lived in the house with a front lawn by the bridge in St. John's Road. Mrs. Harrow organised Sunday Schools there and the knitting of coats for babies. There was a disabled daughter that used to be pushed around in a long 'basket' on wheels." *Joan Butler*

St. Bridget's choir in the church gardens

Father Christmas alias Ken Cooper at All Saints

The Catholic Ladies Group - mid 1950's

Helen Cooper supervises a stall at All Saints fair

Tony McManus' first communion at St. Bridget's

37

The Story of Isleworth

and its Parish Church

(All Saints)

50p

The Parish of Isleworth

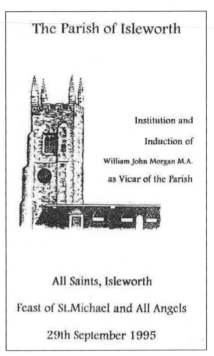

Institution and

Induction of

William John Morgan M.A.

as Vicar of the Parish

All Saints, Isleworth

Feast of St.Michael and All Angels

29th September 1995

*St. Vincent De Paul church
Witham Road*

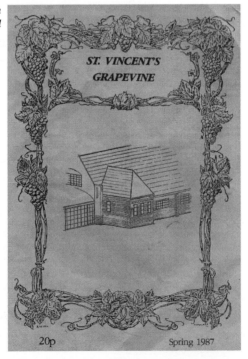

ST. VINCENT'S
GRAPEVINE

20p   Spring 1987

chapter seven
Hitler and Us

Isleworth suffered much war damage

- The first bombs fell on 22nd September 1940 in Borough Road College grounds
- Over 300 incendiary and ten high explosive bombs landed 10th October 1940, six of the latter failed to explode
- The worst raid on 25th August 1944 damaged 550 houses
- Four bombs landed during the 1944 flying bomb period

The **Reporter**
Official Organ of
The Borough of Heston & Isleworth Civil Defence Association.
Affiliated to:— Middlesex Federation of C.D. Associations
National Federation of C.D. Associations
Thames Valley Theatre Guild

| No. 17 | April 1948 | Gratis. |

FLASH BACK No. 5

Photo by kind permission of S. Maurice Evans M.B.E., A.R.I.B.A.
August 29th 1944
Flying Bomb at North Street, Isleworth.

"The memories go on and on... doodlebugs overhead and landing on Silverhall Street. Ferry House ablaze from a bomb. An unexploded one landed at Con Dargon's ferry so we were bombed out for a week, fearing for our cat getting lost or being hungry. Needn't have worried at all, other bombs which landed in the river had thrown up *an ample supply of fish!*" Mary Price

"When the doodlebug went over, I was fishing with the boy next door on the Duke of Northumberland's river and I ran home to the shelter." *Terry Percival*

"We couldn't have shelters in our gardens because of the river flooding so used to sleep in the one they put under the silo. It was a huge concrete thing, must have been reinforced because it was *the devil's own job* to take down when it was eventually demolished." *Jean Lagden*

"They had air-raid shelters in St John's Park. We went down every night, had our own bunk beds. *Used to think they were exciting times*. The night a bomb dropped in Hartland Road, we were down the shelter. When we came up the next

V.E DAY CELEBRATIONS SILVERHALL STREET

morning all the windows in Linkfield Road were gone, blown out. There was a bomb in Smallberry Avenue - one of our neighbours, she is still alive, her father was killed, a direct hit on the house." *Josie Best*

"My friends went into the army, except me. I volunteered for the navy but because I worked on the land, providing food, they wouldn't let me go. I was working for Mr. Lewis, the market gardener in Park Road where Snowy Fielder Way is now. He also had a place at Mogden Lane, Bulls Field by the Rugby Ground" *Ray Farnden*

"During air raids I would sleep under the kitchen table. On the night our cottage in Worple Road was demolished I was buried *under the rubble* for two hours. What I can't understand is how I was got out from the table facing the opposite way to how I went in and slept." *Ken Norman*

"We spent a lot of time in the air-raid shelter when I was at Worple Road School but by the time I went to Smallberry the bombing had lessened. As you came into the school opposite the hospital, down the alleyway to the side of the caretaker's house that is still there, the shelters were just inside the playing fields. I do remember we were in school when the V2 rocket fell on Packards. It killed a lot of people." *Paul Turner*

"We were evacuated which was lucky as our house got bombed. After the war we used to play in the bombed out buildings, there was a lot of vandalism." *Peter Farmer*

"When the air raid sirens went off we all had to file into the shelters dug on the playing field at the corner of Worton and Twickenham Roads. Several of us *did not like being underground* (the word claustrophobic was never used). Gumley was lucky and only had an outside small chapel destroyed by a bomb." *Lorna Newman*

"I remember lying in bed and seeing German planes caught in the search lights, listening for ack-ack/bombing/a crash. A bomb fell on Queen Mary's maternity block at West Middlesex hospital; *the blast blew in our front door* in Amhurst Gardens - you can still see the consequent repairs made by my father. There was an

Anderson shelter in the garden, I helped my father dig it - many nights were spent there." *Leslie Wrangles*

"A string of anti-personnel bombs fell along the Lion Gate in London Road. No one was hurt and there was no resulting damage." *Tommy White*

"During the war a friend's mother lived in North Street and a doodlebug dropped in Hartland Road. Her house was wrecked and all the windows were blown out of our house." *Alice Phipps*

"I don't remember the old Kidd's mill ever working. It was a big black gloomy looking place. It was pulled down during the war because *it was a fire risk*. There was quite a lot of bombing. One of the worst was the London Road opposite Teesdale Avenue or Gardens. We were down the shelter, it's a good job we were. Several bombs fell and the houses were absolutely blown to bits." *Lionel Watson*

"As our hall at the Green School had been bombed we spent our days between the Busch Corner building and the annexe, formerly the County School, in St. John's Road. Monday assemblies were held alternatively at each place, then half of us would walk back to our 'own building' for the day." *Pauline Betts*

"We used to get up the top of the house and watch the planes coming over. I saw the one that come and blew up Magdala Road – buzz bomb. Bombs dropped just at the back of Spring Grove Junior, right behind our garden. They came Sunday morning, gave us two hours to get out so they could dig up *an unexploded bomb* - it stood in the yard of the Milford Arms, big as a pillar box, for years. I think they must have moved it now."

"Another bomb in Star Road, completely demolished that. They gave us 10 minutes to get out; we had to walk down the road with Sunday dinner in pots. The youngest child was in a pram with a big gas mask. We went to relations in Linkfield Road, my old

The clock tower war memorial - unveiled in 1922, renovated 2002

grandmother, and stayed there that night when another raid was on. I was next door *playing on a little pool table* with a couple of friends. There was an aerial torpedo, it hit Smallberry Avenue, just past the Red Lion, blew six or eight houses down – that was the next night, they was following us!" *John Benn*

"We slept in the cellar. A landmine landed opposite our house, we had to move out for three days. In the front room we had some rather nice old shutters but of course they were ruined by the vibration." *Joan Temple*

"We had large air raid shelters in the field of the school in Ridgeway Road – many of our lessons were carried on in there." *Bert Kendall*

THE FERRY HOUSE

On the night 25/26th September 1940, 30 incendiary bombs fell on Taylor's Yard Church Street, Park Road, Isleworth and London Road, Brentford End. This burned down Ferry House. After the war it was rebuilt to as near the original as possible.

"My parents, Harry and Isabella Creak, bought 219 Worton Road in 1938 and we three children were brought up there. Mum's mother also lived with us. During the war father served in The Honourable Artillery Company. Four soldiers from the searchlight crew in Redlees Park were billeted at the house and had the downstairs front room for their use." *June Nesbitt*

chapter eight
Cause for Celebration

Chestnut Grove Golden Jubilee street party - 2002

Charter Day (October 1932) Celebrating Incorporation of the Borough of Heston & Isleworth. "Every child was given a special mug. The morning was spent at school and we were given tickets for free rides at Beech's Fun Fair during the afternoon." *Mary Huxley*

Empire Day (24th May)
It was a big day at Worple Road School. I think Mr. Lugg, the headmaster, must have loved organising. Once, he and some of his top boys painted a *large map of the world* in the playground. Some pupils represented countries on the map, with red, white and blue ribbons round their necks and holding a cardboard box containing articles from each country. As we marched around, we sang National songs." *Laura Hubbard*

"Scouts and Guides could wear their uniforms. Others wore a white shirt or blouse and every child was given a Union Jack flag. We lined up in the playground and sang songs such as Jerusalem and Rule Britannia. *We got the afternoon off.*" *Mary Huxley*

"When I was at Spring Grove Junior, we would all either put on our best dress or dress up in some way. We'd parade in the playground to tambourines and other instruments. I'm not musical and *got to play the triangle*, because I couldn't go too far wrong with that." *Margaret Collins*

Martyrs' Procession
"It was a big day, held for Richard Reynolds. There were bands, and all the schoolchildren took part. We wore veils. It started at St. Bridget's went down South Street, Church Street, Park Road round to the left into the Twickenham Road and into the gardens at Gumley where we had a service. My own children took part in later years. What a shame it's not held now." *Theresa Turner*

"We used to look out of the top bedroom windows and watch the Catholic procession go along. People dressed their windows with flowers and crosses and the Priest used to come along and bless them all." *Alice Phipps*

"Hundreds of people would take part. The Police held up the traffic. Agnes O'Connell and Her All Girls' band all dressed in Irish green uniforms. Agnes would pound a massive drum and lead the procession. All the different organisations had sashes. They'd carry statues, held them high - they must have been tough. Another band was half way down the procession to keep the music going. The weather was always good. We had hymn sheets and held rosaries. We used to sing Faith of Our Fathers – this was the Martyrs' hymn. At the end we would go into Gumley grounds for a fairly short service, benediction, and refreshments. *Agnes would play gigs and reels* – there was an Irish atmosphere." *Kathleen McManus*

A Catholic procession leaves Nazareth House

And Other Religious Processions

"There were always Catholic processions. They'd go from St. Bridget's to Nazareth House. This was an orphanage then. We used to have some of the children home to tea." *Kathleen McManus*

Horse Parade

"We'd look forward to the horse parade, it was really long, all the way up through the high street, *all sorts of carts, old drays*, Watneys' horses up and down the London Road, really was

May Day for the children of the Blue School - 1920

44

something. Around 1937 and after, possibly during the war, went on for many years, every year." *John Benn*

May Day

"We always celebrated May Day in St. John's Park, singing patriotic songs. All schools worked together, the Town, St. Mary's, the Blue School." *Rosemary Chatfield*

Guy Fawkes Night (5th November)

"It was always a big event. Lighting the fireworks only happened on that one night but the preparation was immense. There'd be a bonfire on The Dump. The Mayger family had one somewhere down by the willow tree on the allotment. There'd be a big bonfire in the middle of Worton Road Estate and the Phipps would have their own fabulous one. A month before there would be this build up of rubbish – old furniture and anything. But, because we kids had to go home by half past six, there was always a fear that *someone would nick our bonfire*. These fires were just communal events – no one organised them apart from the kids and on the night people would come along with bangers and jumping jacks and hurl them at each other. There were no safety regulations then." *Don Hughes*

Opening of Twickenham Bridge 1933

"All the children were taken to witness the opening by the Prince of Wales. I was banned from this trip and made my own way there and stood apart from my classmates. *The Prince saw me and waved* so I got one over my teacher and was the envy of the other children." *Leslie Lee*

H M King George V Coronation 1911

"My first visit to Syon was on the occasion of the coronation, when the Duke held a party for all local children. It was held in the Riding School, I was only seven but can remember, we all came home with an orange and a mug." *Tommy White*

H M King George V Jubilee 1935

"I was at Marlborough School, we all got a tin of toffees with the Royal couple on the lid and a local baker gave us a box containing cakes." *Mary Huxley*

H M King George V Memorial Service 1936

"In those days the entrance to All Saints was at the front. My mother was a Methodist and we never

S. T. Cousins

Borough of
HESTON AND ISLEWORTH

THIS BOOK
IS GIVEN TO YOU BY
THE
MAYOR AND CORPORATION
AS A SOUVENIR
OF THE
JUBILEE *of* KING GEORGE V
6TH MAY, 1935

45

ISLEWORTH

SOUVENIR OF H.M.QUEEN ELIZABETH II SILVER JUBILEE 1977

Catalogue 20p

Festival '82

ISLEWORTH PARISH CHURCH

Thurs 12th- Sat 14th August
20p

went there, except just once, for the funeral memorial service." *Lionel Watson*

H M The Queen Coronation 1952
"We went on a special day's outing to Windsor Great Park and the Borough of Heston and Isleworth gave us all a commemorative book about The Queen. I was just nine and very royalist. It was a day to wear my new red, white and blue dress; watch TV around the *small black and white screen* at a neighbour's house with the rest of the street, and have fairy cakes with red, white and blue icing on." *Rosemary Pettersson*

H M The Queen Silver Jubilee 1977
"We had a wonderful party in Silverhall Street with decorated tables all the way down, games in Silverhall Park and Jubilee mugs for the children. In the evening there was music and dancing. *The Pearly King and Queen* attended." *Audrey Morris*

"During 1976 the late Kenneth Cooper approached me about mounting an exhibition on Isleworth's history. A committee was subsequently formed and the resulting event entitled 'Isleworth: The Years Between' presented sculptures, engravings, drawings, paintings, postcards and photographs from the reign of Queen Elizabeth I to Queen Elizabeth II. It's estimated 3,000 people visited it over the ten days." *Andrea Cameron*

Isleworth Parish Church Festival 1982
In All Saints Long Room were paintings by local artists available for purchase,

pottery by Caroline Morcom and Dejah Collier, and glass engravings by Eileen Sheridan. Several local churches exhibited floral arrangements and Thursday was rounded off with a ploughman's supper. Friday saw tours of the church tower and bells under Harold Rogers' direction, and Saturday, walks by Andrea Cameron. (Sundial Parish Magazine)

H M The Queen Golden Jubilee 2002
"The September sky was overcast but Isleworth's riverfront was *a blaze of colour.* Royal Watermen formed a guard of honour, and Thames Watermen, resplendent in red uniforms, held their oars aloft to salute HRH The Duke of York when he named the eight-oared shallop, The Jubilant. After the ceremony, accompanied by a flotilla of cutters in ceremonial rig, it headed a river pageant on its way to Greenwich." *Christine Diwell*

HRH The Duke of York names 'The Jubilant'

"Like many others, Grainger Road's party was held 3rd June. The street was a mass of bunting and flags, as well as there being a bouncy castle, more an animal, which it was difficult to get the children off. To start proceedings a long standing resident cut a ribbon where the road was blocked off. Unable to decide which fancy dress was the winner, every child was given a jubilee mug. The bit I liked best was the magician, *he pulled a white rabbit* from a hat and let the children pat it." *Mary Brown*

Postman's Retirement 2002
"To celebrate Alan Newport's 60th birthday/ retirement and repay many kindnesses over 37 years delivering post in Isleworth, residents of five streets decided to hold a

Alan Newport's birthday

party. The Explorers' Club loaned their hall, over 200 people brought ample food and drink, a cake was cut, speeches given, and a cheque of £876 handed over. The best part was to see people of all ages and ethnic backgrounds mingling happily together."
Christine Diwell

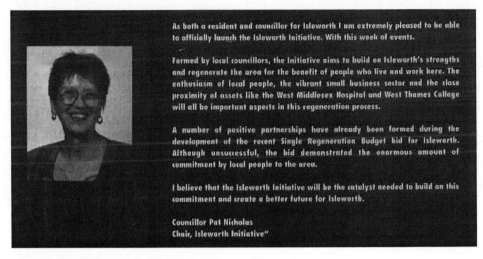

As both a resident and councillor for Isleworth I am extremely pleased to be able to officially launch the Isleworth Initiative. With this week of events.

Formed by local councillors, the Initiative aims to build on Isleworth's strengths and regenerate the area for the benefit of people who live and work here. The enthusiasm of local people, the vibrant small business sector and the close proximity of assets like the West Middlesex Hospital and West Thames College will all be important aspects in this regeneration process.

A number of positive partnerships have already been formed during the development of the recent Single Regeneration Budget bid for Isleworth. Although unsuccessful, the bid demonstrated the enormous amount of commitment by local people to the area.

I believe that the Isleworth Initiative will be the catalyst needed to build on this commitment and create a better future for Isleworth.

Councillor Pat Nicholas
Chair, Isleworth Initiative"

The launch of Isleworth Initiative Week - February 1996

chapter nine
Going to the Fair

The earliest known fair was for two days in Whit Week 123l. Discontinued at the time of the Second World War, it was revived for a few years in the mid-1980s.

The Old Time

"A large fair was held stretching from Upper to Lower Square into a large open space behind a building next to the Northumberland Arms public house and the Kidd's Mill unloading dock. I think it was held first week in July, for most of the week, until the 2nd World War started. After the war, in an attempt not to lose the rights to hold the event, *one local man opened one stall* each year for several years." *Tom Black*

"It was held annually in Phoenix Yard by the Northumberland Arms. In front of Mr. Evan's stables *there would be a coconut shy* and a roundabout would fill the second yard. Beech's fair would be in Lower Square." *John Beal*

"Another interesting event was the fair, held on 1st July and looked forward to so eagerly by all my chums and myself. What happy days we spent there. I expect a lot of children played truant that day. In Phoenix Yard there stood the huge roundabouts and swings. My father was good to us, he always put *a shilling each* on the mantelpiece as he left for work, so we could go to the fair after school." *Laura Hubbard*

"We'd always come down to the fair each year, always looked forward to it - they used to have the swing boats there." *Josie Best*

"Of course one remembers the old time fairs early in July every year – Mr. and Mrs. Evans of North Street's caravan was always there." *Mrs. E.Woodland*

"All round Church Street where I used to live has completely changed. The old girls' Blue School was at the back of the Northumberland Arms where the 37 buses stopped. Yearly they had a fair that went all along the road down to the waterside. From the Swan to the Church. They stopped all the traffic and the buses. It ran

for about three days. It was wonderful, and us kids used to love it – with the confetti and water spouts and old roundabout going. Beech's were the fair people. It was an Isleworth custom." *Eileen Lucas*

And the New

For a few years in the mid-1980s a June Village Fair was staged. Similarly what was called the Isleworth People's Festival took place on the Green, on August Bank Holiday, the first being opened by Hounslow's Mayor Jim Kenna. Attractions included a visit by harmonica player Larry Adler; Helen Cooper remembers selling an African Violet to his wife.

The sun shone for the 1986 Fair when the Isleworth Society stall made nearly £20 profit. But it was not so kind for the Festival, Andrea Cameron recalls "we took a stall and mounted a display of old photographs. It was very windy with squally showers, Liz Welch and I spent the day keeping the display screens upright and covering and uncovering them with large sheets of polythene."

"The first one in which I became involved after moving here, I donated a bottle of whiskey to The Isleworth Society for their raffle. From another stall I won a beautiful Victorian dressed doll which my 16 year old grand-daughter still treasures." *Pam Booth*

Clowning around: Double act Caroline Van der Vlies and Chris Gurney Champion, alias 'Double Dutch', delight the crowd with their antics.

"St. John's Residents Association took part in the Festival. One year we sold home made goods and another time borrowed equipment, from a local Scout group, to run a coconut shy.

This proved popular with young and old alike." *Christine Diwell*

"When we first arrived, after completion of much of the Speyhawk development, a fair was being held on the Green. There were stalls, music and dance demonstrations. *We assumed it would happen every year.* In fact after one more it was abandoned – the space was insufficient and us newcomers weren't yet ready to enter into the spirit of the thing." *John Ray*

Redlees Park - the lettering was added in 1999

Isleworth's LA Fitness - the one-time location of the late Princess Diana's workouts

Spring Grove Allotment and Garden Association at Smith's Garden Party

chapter ten
leisure time

Smith's Garden Party
"A very enjoyable annual event with assorted stalls and tombolas. My young sister was thrilled when she once *won a china tea service*. Mr. and Mrs. Smith employed a reduced sized military band to fit their smaller space. The playing was excellent with a mixture of military music and tunes. Needless to say they were a great attraction to the local 'gals'." *Iris Evans*

Cinema
"I remember the Odeon being built. Worked there later as a projectionist up in the box – not very exciting when you have got to watch *Jane Eyre for a fortnight!*" *John Benn*

Eden Agencies Ltd.

OFFER YOU A COMPLETE SERVICE FOR YOUR

TRAVEL & HOLIDAY REQUIREMENTS

6, Odeon Parade, London Road, Isleworth   560 8002.

"I was a member of the Mickey Mouse Saturday Club at the Odeon. When it was a girl's birthday she got a toy tea set made from tin. The usherettes had a busy time *sorting out the rowdies*. When the projector broke down the noise of shouting and foot stamping was horrific." *Joan Butler*

"Two unusual trips were made to the Odeon – all pupils from the local secondary schools assembled to see the classic Henry V with Laurence Oliver, and also The Great Mr. Handel. They are vivid memories." *Pauline Betts*

Isleworth Explorers Boys Club (Affiliated to the Middlesex Association of Boys' Clubs) Twickenham Road, Isleworth 560-4552 Leader Mr. S. Bennett This is a new purpose built club which will be open from 1st June 1969

Scouts
"Mr. Dicky White was Scoutmaster at All Saints Church, assisted by the Rev. Rowton and Mr. Somerfield, the Curate. Activities were held in the St. John's Rec, the church hall in South Street and a little

room in Hartland Road. We once had a camp in Marble Hill grounds." *John Beal*

"My father was involved with the 1st Isleworth Scouts from when they started, must have been around 1912, so I had no option but to join. We met at the Town School. Mother and father helped to put on pantomimes at Marlborough School – the Cubs and Scouts took part - the costumes were made of crepe paper. Mr. Imber was Scout Master. He had an old Ford car and once took us off to see over an old aircraft, eight of us at a time, it was a great experience." *Keith Knight*

Isleworth Rowing Club
"The headquarters were in Finn's boathouse outside the London Apprentice. I was a member of a rowing eight. We raced in regattas at Teddington, Richmond and Kingston." *John Beal*

You can always depend on
RADIO · TELEVISION
OR
ELECTRICAL APPLIANCES
Purchases from
WADDEN AND **HILL** LIMITED
459-461, London Road, Isleworth.   44, High Street, Hounslow.
ISLEW 33491   HOUN 1724

Wireless
"I sat on the stairs in the dark, when I was supposed to be in bed, *listening to ITMA* - a very popular radio comedy programme in 1948. I believe it had been running during the war." *Pam Strickland*

"We used to take the accumulator to be charged. Had to make sure it was on full power for granny to listen to Henry Hall and his band." *Joan Butler*

the Old Isleworth festival
...music at the river's edge

24th - 29th June
1997

£1

Political meetings
"In the late '20s and '30s even the wireless was not very common. One source of entertainment was political meetings held outdoors in front of the King's Arms (the area was larger before the street widening) or indoors in the Public Hall for special occasions. They were notorious for members of the opposite party putting 'catch questions' to *inexperienced candidates* who often had to be 'rescued' by their political agents sitting next to them." *Arthur Wenden*

South West Middlesex Music Festivals
"During the 1940s, choirs, musicians and speakers from the upper forms of local grammar schools assembled for these day long events. The

conductor was always Mrs. Swann, a great friend of our Green School music mistress Miss Hare, and her stepson Donald Swann *(of Flanders and Swann fame)* was the accompanist. He sometimes came along to our school rehearsals." *Pauline Betts*

Isleworth Festival of Music & Dance
This is our fifth year and we hope you will enjoy all that is on offer. Virtuoso pianist, Joanna MacGregor, and award winning actress Jenny Agutter are amongst those performing. Add to this the renowned Rambert Dance Company and you can see why the festival is fast gaining a national reputation for its ground breaking work. Festival Programme, 10-21st May 2000

Theatre – at Isleworth Public Hall Isleworth Actors' Company
"Isleworth is full of professional actors, directors and other stage people. Most of the time they're not working in the way they wish. *One day on 'The Bill'* every six months is hardly job satisfaction when you're wanting to play King Lear. Our idea was, it would be nice to set up something like the old fashioned reps, where you had a mixture of experienced actors playing decent roles as well as possible, and mix them with young graduates from drama schools. Recruitment complete, we announced we

were going to play in the spring and it would be The Tempest. Some people were pleased, some horrified. It all worked very well. It was a lot of fun. We followed it with Tartuffe in Autumn 1999, building on our success." *Arthur Horwood*

The Stop Gap Theatre Company is here again following our sojourn at the Paul Robeson Theatre. Being at Isleworth carries advantages, like having the time and access to build an ambitious set, being able to run our own bar and creating our own informal seating arrangements. Lend Me a Tenor programme 2002

Informal Theatre

"The International Friendship Club used to put on pantos and do extracts from Blithe Spirits and the like. We put on one show for the League of Friends at West Middlesex Hospital. It was a great mistake to time it after they had had their meal and a couple of drinks – *most of the audience fell asleep!*" Ann Cooke

Making Music

"The picture of the band in the 1950s shows Les Donald on drums, Eddie Bowry, bass. Jim Corney was the singer, with Bill Bowry on piano and me with the guitar."

"By the 1970s we were called Part Four – I was the singer and played guitar. My two sons Jack and David were on drums and bass guitar, with Paul Ackerman of Mill Plat Avenue making up the fourth. This was the best band I was with, we had great times together, I was sorry when we had to give it up." *Ray Farnden*

Walking

"We had been given ten wonderful years after Margaret was confined to a wheelchair - to work together, write "walks" books, and help various organisations to do with disability. It was entirely suitable that after her death Margaret's greatest achievement,

Harry Goddard's Rhythm Dance Band mid-1930's

56

a complete book of ten wheelchair accessible riverside walks, was given its publishing launch in the Conservatory at Syon House." *John Ray*

Park perfection

Swimming
"Many a crocodile of children walked from the Blue School to the baths for their weekly lessons – a few of the most able had extra sessions. This bore fruit in 1961 when the boys' team won the championship of the old Borough of Heston and Isleworth." *Arthur Spikins*

Parks
"What is now Redlees Park used to be Greenham's gravel pits. The firm was a large set up, excavated gravel and sand - it was washed and graded then a large fleet of lorries carried it away. When all the gravel was worked out it became a landfill site. *They came and dumped London trams there*, put them in a pit and set fire to them, the amount of burning was fantastic. Metal would be salvaged, the rest went into the ground. The same happened with buses. Later the site was topped off with soil and made into a park." *Bert Kendall*

"I seem to think that Redlees recreation ground was, at first, only open on Saturdays." *Leslie Lees*

Roller Skating
"If you couldn't afford a bike, you had roller skates. Those who were lucky had ball bearings, but if you only had ordinary wheels you had to put more effort into it. There was a whole gang of us. One of them, Clarke, *was a real daredevil.* He went ever so fast and got stopped by the Police once for breaking the speed limit! At that time it was 10 m.p.h. I think." *Arthur Wenden*

Holidays at Home/Isleworth Community Association
"Because no-one could go away to the seaside during the war years the idea came about of Holidays at Home. All sorts of groups – music appreciation, a

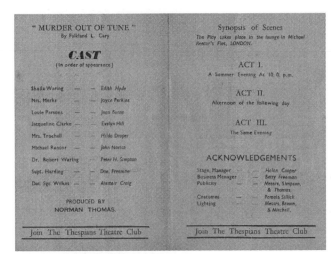

choir, ladies sewing class, photographic and drama – met, mainly in schools, each one well attended. I remember the Over 60s Club was really thriving. Eventually this all somehow became Isleworth Community Association."

"As part of this, in 1949 I was 'volunteered' as stage manager for 'Murder Out of Tune' at Marlborough Senior School although I knew nothing about the job. We had a great carnival that year. Lots of us processed round Isleworth on floats. The drama group did a scene from Macbeth. I was

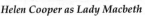
Helen Cooper as Lady Macbeth

Lady Macbeth, wearing a ruby coloured gown. There I was sitting on the throne surrounded by handsome courtiers.

I'd just drunk the poison so was not looking too well. All of us were trying to be serious, but as we came round the corner a large lady was standing there and she suddenly called out to one of our group, "Hey Bill, did you get the bread then"? Of

*Ken Cooper surrounded by
Miss Isleworth contestants*

58

course we collapsed with laughter. Jimmy Knode, the bookie, he hired a four in hand carriage and drove round looking splendid in top hat and morning dress. The local doctor, Dr. Jouhar, was a great photographer and put on an exhibition of photos at Isleworth Library. The events ended with a dance held at Marlborough. A Beauty Queen was chosen and she was attended by the Toni (home perm) Twins from Gillettes." *Helen Cooper*

Miss Isleworth 1949

Miss Isleworth 1949
flanked by the Toni (home perm) Twins

Miss Isleworth 1949:
let the carnival dance begin!

ISLEWORTH COMMUNITY ASSOCIATION
presents

PALACE OF VARIETIES

By kind permission of the

B. B. C.

Real old time Variety where the audience
joins in the fun

MARLBOROUGH SCHOOL
SATURDAY, 10th JANUARY

Doors open 7.45 p.m.   Curtain 8 p.m.

Tickets
2/6

Special Price for
Children. TICKETS 1/-

The stained glass window adorning the 1999 extension

chapter eleven
Isleworth Public Hall

Subscriptions were raised in 1887 to add a Public Hall to the existing 1863 building containing the Vestry and Reading Rooms.

Learning to Swim

Built at the rear of the Public Hall the baths opened 1873 having cost £1456, closing 1880. Messrs. Wisdom Brothers submitted the only tender for alterations costing £685 in 1903 and the baths subsequently re-opened. On 26th August 1939 new premises costing some £44,500 opened in the Twickenham Road. Leslie Wrangles remembers having an annual season ticket costing two shillings and sixpence. The 2002 price for a single swimming session was £2.55, with a 40p reduction for Leisure Card holders.

"One of the highlights was swimming which in those days was only in Summer time. The water was *inhabited by cockroaches* alive and dead and, as you undressed in cubicles, out they would come around your feet. Mr. Collier, the attendant, would place a webbing belt around your waist on a long length of rope and drag you round." *Laura Hubbard*

"The swimming pool itself, small and unhygienic though it was, played a great part in the teaching of swimming either through school parties or individually. The water was, I believe, only changed once a week and on Fridays *you could hardly see the bottom*." *Arthur Wenden*

"It was a 50 feet length baths used by the local schools as well as the general public. I, like many of the local children before the war, have a certificate for passing swimming tests at the baths." *Tom Black*

"I used to come to the swimming club down the alleyway. There was no heated water, it was perishing cold. We'd come on Tuesdays and Thursdays and then the boys came on Mondays and Fridays. It was three half pence. In later years they did provide hot Bovril if you paid for it." *Eileen Lucas*

Swimming Baths at rear of Public Hall

"Aged about seven I was going regularly for swimming lessons at the baths situated behind the Public Hall, with Margaret Lillyman, elder daughter of the butcher on the London Road. A cousin of hers, Mollie Bradley, taught at the Blue School and took Margaret and me to the baths. With a belt round our waist, to which *a long rope* was attached, Mollie walked along the side of the bath giving us instructions."
Grace Cousins

"I attended swimming classes and completed the Murray test. This covered three lengths of the baths freestyle, also three breast stroke and three on your back. When you had passed, you became a helper assisting new learners. Admission fees were one and a half pence for juniors, three pence for seniors, and four pence on Sundays."
John Beal

"Went from school to the baths to learn to swim. There was a boardwalk covered with coconut matting around the bath with changing cubicles all round. Men and boys swam at different times to the women and girls." *Leslie Wrangles*

"The baths were still at the back of the Public Hall in 1953." *Sheila Hance*

The Library
The front of the Public Hall opened as a Vestry and Reading Room in 1863 providing 1400 volumes; a librarian's room and store were added 1871. In 1904 the Reading Room became Isleworth Public Library. 1931 opening hours were 9 a.m – 9 p.m.

"An exciting thing was the library, which my sister and I made good use of. One book was allowed at a time for which you paid a penny. All the books were covered in a dark blue cover, which made the library look most depressing – so different from today, with colourful covers and pleasant surroundings. We enjoyed collecting one book a week, particularly as Grandma - who could not read or write - would not encourage books in our house *saying they were devil's work* and stopped you doing useful things." *Laura Hubbard*

"Charles Ravenhill, the tailor, doubled as part time librarian. The application form to join had to be signed by a ratepayer. Customers stood at a counter and chose books from a list provided. Books were stored in locked glass cabinets and customers were not allowed near them." *Tommy White*

"You could not look at the books but were given a list of titles to choose from. The library held a personal record book, in which was recorded books taken in and out." *John Beal*

Mayor Alderman G.R. Speed presided when purpose built premises in the Twickenham Road opened 10th October 1936. Pam Strickland recalls: "The library was very important to me, I was there every other day or so, being what my mother said was a bookworm." Current ticket holders are allowed 10 books at any one time for a renewable period of 28 days.

Going to the Pictures

"Another feature was the Bijou or Picture House. *Oh! what bliss*, for every Saturday afternoon this is where all the children gathered to see Pearl White or Houdini, two famous stars who were in lengthy serials each week. If you could afford four pence then you sat on red plush seats at the back and itched all the way home. Otherwise for one penny you sat on wooden chairs." *Laura Hubbard*

"My first recollections of the Public Hall were Saturday morning film shows put on by a travelling projectionist in the upstairs hall for which we paid, I believe, tuppence. We sat on long benches and enjoyed such silent characters as Charlie Chaplin, Tom Mix (the cowboy), *Dr. Fu Manchu* and a robot called 'The Iron Man' who used to dispose of his enemies by a violent mailed fist on to their heads. There was nearly always a serial, which finished each weekly episode with the hero or heroine in some critical crisis making it imperative to go the next week to see how it was resolved. As there were always some in the audience who could not read the captions to the films, one frequently heard the words "What's it say"? during the performances." *Arthur Wenden*

The Public Hall circa 1960

Formal cinema facilities closed 14th October 1921 while the Odeon, designed by George Coles and seating 1600, did not open in the London Road until March 1935. It closed 5th January 1957, subsequently becoming Isleworth Studios and is now divided into residential accommodation. Today's cinema

goers have to travel to the multi-screen complexes in nearby Richmond or Feltham.

Attending Meetings

Various projects for the disposal of county sewage were discussed and a resolution was agreed, to be moved at a public meeting 12th February. *Isleworth Citizen, March 1930*

Forty or more years ago, when Blue School Governors met in the Vestry Room, some Governors had to retire at the end of three years and election to fill vacancies was simply by a show of hands. At a Town's Meeting any ratepayer was entitled to vote. The first meeting I went to there were only 17 present. As people became to realise its importance more and more attended until it was not possible for even the Public Hall to hold them. Eventually the Charity Commissioners agreed to the Town Council nominating people to fill vacancies. Albert Turner, Sundial Parish Magazine

The launch of the Isleworth Municipal Restaurant

Eating

"Because of food rationing, school dinners were served at the government-run 'British Restaurant' in South Street." *Cecilia Whelan*

"After 1943 I used the upstairs or working persons' canteen. A

64

three course meal, with a choice of menu, for 9d (today not quite 4p). On the ground floor was the school canteen and dinners were two courses for only 6d (today 2p). I heard many derogatory words about the latter and certainly *the smell was most uninviting.*"
Lorna Newman

"Mother was a server in the British Restaurant, she helped in the school holidays. Meals cooked there were meat and two veg with plum duff to follow, for sixpence." *Joan Hazell*

Professional Theatre

"It was Allison Hancock who started the Isleworth Actors' Company. She came to me one day and said, "Look, you know all this fuss about them trying to pull down the Public Hall, well, I think it would be an ideal place for a fringe theatre". I said, "Well, I don't". But Allison's the sort of person who's a bit irresistible at times, so, although I thought it a daft idea, I went along with it. We joined the Steering Group. Got bogged down with all the stuff that was going on there. It was a strange experience, but the woman from Community Initiative Partnerships leading it was very interesting. I spoke to her after a meeting, told her about Allison's idea and said I didn't think it would work. But she said, "I do". We arranged to meet. She had a very imaginative approach. And so we started work."
Arthur Horwood

Parties and the Like

"It was a centre for frequent dances, wedding functions and parties often using Mrs. Brown, who kept the confectioner shop further down the street towards the fountain, as caterers. It was where I started 'Old Tyme' dancing classes in the 1950s"
Arthur Wenden

"My memory was going to the brewery children's parties in the late '20s and '30s and after the war in the late '40s and '50s helping to run dances and gang shows for the Scouts. As for the dances, the

65

thing I remember most was we had a drinks' licence until 11 p.m. and the public houses closed at 10.30, so we had some fun trying to *keep the gatecrashers out* for the last half hour." *Tom Black*

"My recollection is attending B.P. Scout Guild dances run by the 3rd Osterley Rovers." *Stephen Randall*

"I met my husband there in 1936. There were dances every Saturday, run by Mr. and Mrs. Tucker. Entry was one shilling. One week the band would be John Skim and His Boys and the next it would be Reggie's Rhythm Band. *The hall was lit by gas lamps*." *Gwen Burnham*

"We used to go to the brewery children's Christmas party. Mr. Phillips played the piano." *Joan Butler*

The hall was a riot of colour for the Isleworth & District Horticultural Society Summer Show, with over 60 entrants, in classes for flowers, vegetables and home-made produce. Sundial Parish Magazine, 1975

As well as other things…

"One of the rear rooms of the hall was a clinic for expectant mothers and later their babies."

"There were also trade exhibitions such as the one put on in the 1930s by the Council to encourage more consumption of electricity from their power station in Bridge Road, Hounslow. Electric irons, cookers and vacuum cleaners were not in common use at that time. I remember Mr. Nias, the first Mayor of the Borough, opening it and saying that one advantage of the electric cooker over the gas equivalent was that it was no use *putting your head in it* when depressed." *Arthur Wenden*

"Done something different today, went round the Public Hall where they were buying old gold and silver. Took my charms round and a few bits of silver, and a little fob. Asked the man to look at my heavy bracelet, he said I should insure it for £650. This is what it would cost to be replaced. But the actual gold value was £160!" *Mary Jolley's diary, 1st December 1982*

By 1990 the fabric of the building had deteriorated. It was threatened with closure but a successful campaign was mounted for its preservation and restoration. On 9th December 2000 a special event celebrated the addition of a small side extension, a lift and new toilets.

chapter twelve
Syon House

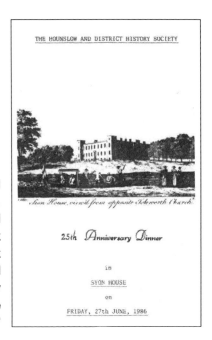

"Early in 1919 my father was called to Syon and asked to take on the contract to wind the clocks. They had not been wound during the war and remained silent. On the second week he took me along, aged 14, to deal with the stable block turret clock. The top of the stables housed wounded soldiers as it was an Auxiliary Military Hospital. There was a man made pond at the rear *where the horses were washed.*" *Tommy White*

"I interviewed Leopold Benn, the Duke's Waterman. He lived at the Lodge and told me a lovely story about the Duke visiting with *a bottle of whiskey at Christmas*. The Duke asked Benn to open it and said he would play his favourite tune on the piano in Benn's living room. It was My Blue Heaven." *Helen Cooper*

"One thing intrigued us kids. Just past the old ferry where Mr. Dargon used to row across, there's a pavilion on the riverbank. When I was a kid there was a sort of underground boathouse there. *In it was an old wooden boat*, very big. There was some sort of barrier, you couldn't get through to it. It had 1914 carved at one end. It was there for years but you could never get in to see what it really was. Eventually it rotted away." *Lionel Watson*

"My father worked as a gardener and we lived in the grounds. In the 1927 flood mum woke in the night thinking the lavatory was overflowing. Father got out of bed up to his knees in water. I was four years' old and came running down the passage and fell into the water

Storm damage at Syon House

67

because I couldn't see the step into the kitchen. We could not open the front door so had to go through a window. My father got me out first and carried me on his shoulder, *my feet dangling in the water*; then he went back to get my mum. We had to live with the head gardener for a fortnight – his house was on higher ground than our bungalow. Syon had a dairy farm but the cows were OK. The pigs and chickens drowned." *Ray Farnden*

Francis Farnden, gardener at Syon House

Debutants at Syon

"Uncle Ted lived at the Lodge on the London Road. Last time I visited, I must have been seven or eight years' old. He took us round the fields with his pockets full of rabbits, just to please the kids." *John Benn*

"In the 1930s no-one saw the grounds except when the Duke and Duchess were in residence and they invited people in. They had huge parties, sometimes with dancing on the lawns, entertained by the famous orchestras of the day." *Ray Farnden*

"Tommy White, who wound and mended the clocks, was allowed to call the 'old' Duke by *his nickname, Nobby*. One day Tommy took me on a tour of the house. We started at 10.00 a.m, went from basement up on to the roof and ended 2.30 p.m. without a break, but still hadn't visited every room." *Andrea Cameron*

"Mum regularly used to take my brother and me for walks – down to the river and then we would go on into Syon *to look at the piglets*, which were on the right hand side beside the path. The cows were milked in the barn where until lately there was the farm shop. They used to sell the milk locally." *Keith Knight*

"The conker season would be just after school went back - we'd get them down in Syon Park. It was quite easy to get in the trees there, and no-one ever stopped us." *Don Hughes*

"We used to go over to Syon Park, it was totally different to now, with a little dirt track to walk through. They had pigs during the war time and would bring the cows across for milking." *Josie Best*

"I did belong to a Pleasant Monday Afternoon Group and through that was lucky enough to be invited by the Duchess of Northumberland to a wonderful tea party. We were asked into her drawing room to see her in the beautiful robes she wore for the coronation of the Queen Mother. *Our tea was all laid out* in the grounds and we all felt so privileged." *Mrs. E. Woodland*

We always planned for our first AGM to be something special and it's certainly going to be just that. As the Public Hall is presently undergoing refurbishment, the Duke kindly offered us free use of the Great Conservatory. Naturally we accepted. Friends of Isleworth Public Hall, Newsletter March 2000

The Friends of Isleworth Public Hall AGM in the Great Conservatory

"When The Hounslow & District History Society celebrated its 21st anniversary with a dinner in the Camellia restaurant, I remarked to the Duke I found it strange he spent his winters in the north where it's usually colder than the south. His reply was that when in late September he was having dinner at Syon with his overcoat on, he knew it was time to go to Alnwick where he had more central heating."

"By contrast, for our Silver Jubilee dinner in the dining room, with once more the Duke and Duchess present, it was such a warm evening the windows were opened to let the scent from the Rose Gardens waft in." *Andrea Cameron*

"The gates were moved back when the entrance was enlarged to cater for the National Garden Centre that opened in 1968. Originally between the two metal gates there was a revolving turnstile for use by pedestrians. I believe this was never locked." *Tommy White*

"It was around 1986 when I first became a Syon guide. I couldn't understand why members of one of the first groups I took round kept going *down on their hands and knees* and looking underneath the furniture – it turned out they were studying antique restoration. In the 11th Duke's time, he lived at the house most of the time - you could hear music, smell the cigarette smoke and chocolate cake for tea." *Margaret Collins*

"You can't, to my knowledge, get a wheelchair up and into the front entrance but Margaret wanted to go inside. We approached tentatively and mentioned our problem. A film crew, who happened to be shooting there, came pouring out. They surrounded the wheelchair and the next thing I saw was Margaret, wheelchair and all, hoisted shoulder high and *carried triumphantly* up the great steps into the house." *John Ray*

Syon Park gates - a linocut by F. Peake, 4A
Smallberry Green School, 1949

The Percy coat of arms - a linocut by
O. Walker, 3B, Smallberry Green School 1949

chapter thirteen
And so to School

The Borough of Heston and Isleworth held an Education Week in June 1936. Among the plethora of information in the Souvenir Handbook was: Make Sure of a Regular Daily Action of the Bowels. Not all food taken can be absorbed into the body – we often take more than necessary. Also there are some parts of food the body does not need. This material passes down the food canal and is finally removed by action of the bowel. If this removal of waste does not take place daily the system becomes clogged, poisonous products are formed and absorbed, and the whole body suffers, e.g. we are all familiar with the peevish, unhappy and often naughty child, whose only trouble is that his bowels are not acting efficiently and regularly.

Infant and Primary Schools

Woodland St. John's Infants, St. John's Road
Originally for 125 children age four to seven, after which they attended either the Blue or Town School, it closed 1973. The building is now divided into two private residences.

"This was my first school, I think the teacher was Miss Tuck. She had a short leg and wore a metal platform on her foot. It terrified us!" *Joan Butler*

"I went there to teach around 1967. The building was a strange layout, three rooms forming an L shape, one for the infant class, behind that another classroom, and to the side a store room. All were served by one joint chimney but each room had its own fireplace with open coal fires in enormous grates - later these were replaced by enormous gas heaters. The two classrooms only had a partition between. With one teacher in each there had to be good discipline, you couldn't make too much noise. There was only an outside toilet of course. The other half of the building, formerly the staff house, was let out." *Margaret Kendall*

Worple Road – now Worple School, Queen's Terrace **A display to mark its 100 years history was mounted in the school hall. The new premises, for 220 pupils, in Queen's Terrace, were built on the extended playing fields of the old school. This £3 million facelift is the pride of the district and opened 27th April 1994.** Ken Cooper, Sundial Parish Magazine, May 1997

Worple Road children at play circa 1954

"On my first day at school, after prayers and a hymn, we were all given what looked like a lid off a biscuit tin and it was filled with sand, and with it we learnt to make our first letters and sums." *Laura Hubbard*

"Mr. Lugg was the headmaster. On my first day of infants, my sister took me in. I was holding a bunch of flowers for the teacher. Evidently I got so bored with the conversation I hit the teacher *around the face with the flowers*. Not a good start!" *Leslie Lees*

"In the bitterly cold winter of 1947, I'd just recovered from a bad bout of chicken pox and, among other things, the toilet block in the playground was frozen. My mother thought it best to keep me away from school - only a day later the School Attendance man knocked at our front door to insist I return immediately." *Ralph Diwell*

"Most children came home to lunch as mums were home more in those days, not having jobs. It was a junior mixed school but we had P.E. separately. I remember taking the 11+ exam, not being at all phased by it - I didn't know its significance, only *a bit put out* because the rest of the school had a holiday." *Pam Strickland*

Friday 30 November Mufti Day – if you would like to come to school in your ordinary clothes (yes you can wear trainers!) you must bring a bottle…a bottle of shampoo, bubble bath, perfume, juice, wine…something you think someone would like to win as a prize! Worple Primary School News, Issue 102, November 2001

Isleworth Blue Church of England Primary, North Street
The history of this remarkable school has been traced from 1630; from charity school to the present system of primary education, including nursery and infant departments. *Gillian Morris, Isleworth Blue School*

The Blue School, Lower Square - linocut by C. Stone, 3C, Smallberry Green School, 1949

Around the 1930s, through charities and bequests, it had a good annual income so the Governors were able to make half-yearly payments of £5 each towards books and clothes of children who had passed grammar school examinations, but whose parents needed financial assistance. They also made grants of £25 to children staying on for further education. Demands became so great that ultimately a means test had to be introduced. Albert Turner, Sundial Parish Magazine

The visit of HRH Princess Marina, Duchess of Kent, 1961

"I remember with affection Dusty Head, the caretaker when the school was in the old building at North Street and Mr. Fairs, the Head, when the school was in Lower Square." *John Beal*

"It was where Percy Gardens is now, when I went there. There was an air raid shelter in front of it. The last 20 feet of ground between the school and river was a *piggery with about 20*

ISLEWORTH BLUE SCHOOL

THE DEDICATION AND LAYING
OF THE FOUNDATION STONE

of the
NEW CHURCH OF ENGLAND PRIMARY SCHOOL

by
THE RIGHT REV. CYRIL EASTAUGH, M.C., M.A.
LORD BISHOP OF KENSINGTON
and
THE REV. EDWARD H. GRIMSTON
VICAR OF ARUNDEL
(Formerly Vicar of the Parish Church of All Saints, Isleworth)

WEDNESDAY, 20th JULY, 1960 at 3 p.m.

The Foundation Stone has been kindly presented and inscribed by Mr. C. J. Finch, a parent of one of the pupils at the Blue School.
The Silver Trowel to be used in the laying of the Foundation Stone has been kindly presented by Mr. Charles Pike, the Architect of the new school.

73

pigs. The kids used to go and feed and look at them." *Terry Percival*

"I don't know whether it was St. George's or May Day, but we used to have a little pageant when I was in the infants. The school had a big forecourt and it was held there. *They'd dress me up as a Welsh girl* – I had one of these tall hats and a little cap underneath.

Blue School pupils, July 1961

I stood there and cried because I didn't like it on my head." *Eileen Lucas*

"In 1957 its front wall formed the boundary with the pavement. There was just a small garden leading to the door of the caretaker's cottage where George Beech reigned supreme. The central hall served as school office and head's study, alongside was a room for the top class. Two 'new' rooms accommodated the youngest infants and a splendidly large one the oldest. First year juniors were in a similar room, leaving just one more. So what of the other two junior classes? Simple answer, build a partition to separate them – a very effective system, if one teacher raised a voice, the other class also took notice. Meals were prepared at the Town School and served from insulated containers." *Arthur Spikins*

"Mrs. Nicholson was headmistress when I taught there. She was something of a martinet and feared *by staff and pupils alike*. We all believed, as she walked to school, she would recite the Lord's Prayer. At whichever point she had reached as she marched into assembly, all the teachers and pupils had to join in." *Margaret Bush*

"I was there from 1953-60, the old school in North Street which was pulled down. It was run by this tyrant of a woman, Mrs. Nicholson. But I loved Christmas there. You knew when it was coming because we'd sing carols in the hall and she would pound the old piano. The climax would be a Christmas party

John May (on recorder) with Mayor Alderman Stephens

74

and we'd all dress up in fancy dress. I used to love this. The toilets were disgusting, outside of course. The boys' loo for having a Jimmy in didn't even have a roof and one prank was to try and pee *over the wall into the allotments*. It was about eight feet high and I don't recall anyone ever doing it!" *Don Hughes*

"Our Christmas festivities were quite spectacular. The partition in the room where I taught was opened to enlarge the hall, every cupboard and shelf was covered over and decorated, making work impossible. Weeks of rehearsal culminated in a spectacular dancing display before visitors and children, most of whom went home to lunch to return in fancy dress." *Pauline Betts*

In many schools uniform has been dispensed with, but this is not so at The Blue School where we consider it of great importance. A uniform means children can identify with and easily be seen to be members of the school. Importance is attached to a smart appearance and children in the Infant and Junior Departments are expected to wear the uniform. Blue School Prospectus 1992

Isleworth Town, Twickenham Road
Opened 30th November 1910. By standards then, the building was excellent, though the heating arrangements so far from good that most early visitors came to inspect the boiler house. Because of the cold, tempers were raised and a 'disrespectful and insubordinate' caretaker reprimanded. But the temperature remained so low that at one time 150 children and five teachers were suffering from chilblains. Heston and Isleworth Schools' Local History Society 29.8.58

"The head announced at assembly that a big delivery of coke was due and all children must stay away from it. At playtime I was fascinated and ran up to the pile, was caught, and *got the cane* as punishment." *Mary Huxley*

"I went to Worple Road but they said "put him in the Town School" – of course I wasn't learning any more there because I couldn't see the words. It was like pulling down a shutter. I was dyslexic but they didn't call it that then." *Eric Brown*

"On my first day I was accosted by a bully but socked him and he left me alone after that. The

Town School infants, 1938

schooling was not good as most teachers went on war duty. The headmaster had a thing about spelling. He would burst into a classroom at any time unannounced, pick out a child and *challenge them to spell a word*. Incorrect spelling earned a whack on the hand with the cane he carried." *Frank Winterborne*

"Apart from assembly lines and roll call, the playground was the social area. Hours were spent playing 'Release-i-o', or joining the girls in a gigantic skip-in with a long rope. That is, when they weren't playing 'Farmer in the Dell'. On wet days *we crowded into the playshed* where we could swap and play flick with cigarette cards. The milk monitor would bring his class's crate of milk in for which we'd pay half a penny. To get at the milk one had to push in the centre of the cardboard top and push in a straw – these were made of real straw, not plastic." *Brian Cullum*

"Mr. Brown was a veteran from the First World War and he'd got one glass eye. From time to time it had to be changed and he'd wear an eye patch then. He was very good, very patriotic. Any anniversary of the war he could tell you what happened." *Lionel Watson*

"Although we lived so close, I was always the last one to school. As a consequence the Headmaster, Mr. Brown, decided he'd *make me the bell monitor* in order to get me in on time. My mother thought that was an absolutely brilliant idea. There was a gang of boys who used to bully the little girls. I'd fight their battles for them." *Joan 'Molly' Brown*

"When I was teaching in the 1950s, the Education Officer, a Mr. Bennett, asked the local Teachers' Visual Aids Society to make a film strip history of Isleworth. It devolved to a teacher from Smallberry Green and myself to do it. Most schools bought a copy entitled 'Isleworth, a Riverside Village'. The notes accompanying it were written by a Mr. Liddicoat, deputy head at Smallberry Green, formerly of the Blue School." *Arthur Wenden*

"There were wooden huts in the playground. The youngest of us had a sleep in the afternoons, on low camp beds - they may have been ex-army as this was about 1948. Miss Blane walked around to make sure we slept, but I never wanted to. She wore a long dress, and stockings with seams and black work at the heels; I always thought *it was a funny thing to wear.*" *Keith Knight*

Spring Grove Junior School
"Then situated in Villiers Road, it was excellent, run by Miss A.B. Harding, a relative of Gilbert Harding of BBC fame, with her second in command, Miss Humphries, and Miss Donovan, in charge of the five year olds. We certainly learned our 3Rs thoroughly, with

regular mental arithmetic and spelling tests, as well as history and geography, nature study and physical exercises. We did little plays, as well as singing, and I recollect one performance when we put on Charles Dickens' Christmas Carol." *Grace Cousins*

Marlborough Infants, London Road entered via Quaker Lane **Opened 29th June 1936 to accommodate 400 infants the building consisted of assembly hall, six standard size, one large classroom and one for babies, necessary administration and medical rooms, cloakrooms, lavatories and storerooms. The contract price was £13,600. In 1953 it began life as a Primary School moving into new purpose built premises on the same site, but accessed from Darcy Road, in February 1997.**

MONDAY, 29th JUNE

OFFICIAL OPENING

of the

MARLBOROUGH INFANTS' SCHOOL
at 10 p.m.

and new

HESTON JUNIOR SCHOOL
at 12 a.m.

by the

Rt. Hon. Oliver Stanley, M.C., M.P.

(President of the Board of Education)

supported by

THE RI WORSHIPFUL THE MAYOR (Alderman G. R. Speed, J.P.)
Aldermen, Councillors, Teachers, Ratepayers and Parents

Busch House Open Air Mixed,
now Syon Park School, Twickenham Road
"This was a special school for delicate children and when you were deemed recovered and fit you left and moved to mainstream. I was there 1949-1953. Pupils were aged five to 14 and open air was seen as a cure. The classrooms were in the grounds, mainly consisting of glass and built on pillars. The sliding doors were always open, even when there was snow on the ground. Miss Burridge was headmistress - if she caught a child wearing a vest she would remove it." *Linda Parris*

"When we got in first thing we had breakfast in the big house at the front. After that we had lessons then lunch. Then we had a sleep. They gave us some malt because we were supposed to be weak and *something called Scott's emulsion*, it was white - I hated it." *John Best*

Secondary Education

"The 5th and 6th forms of the Green School joined up with Spring Grove Grammar and Isleworth County to form an inter-school discussion group. We met about once a term at the different schools. Subsequently we attended dances at Isleworth County and were also invited to those at Borough Road College." *Pauline Betts*

Gumley House Twickenham Road, accessed via St John's Road. **Founded in 1841 by the Faithful Companions of Jesus, in 1993 it was incorporated as a Grant Maintained single sex Roman Catholic day school, having changed in 1966 from being a selective grammar to fully comprehensive.**

The junior study hall, Gumley House

A short history of

GUMLEY HOUSE
1841-1991
150th anniversary
F.C.J.
convent & school

"My first memory of school was at age five in 1932, being taken to call on Reverend Mother. I stood outside the green door awaiting entry, was then conducted inside by a dainty elderly lady, Miss Miller, taken along a colonnaded walk, and into a parlour to await audience."
Cecilia Whelan

"Despite war years and clothes being on ration ALL wore school uniform and we were proud of it. Hats quite often only went on just before entering the school gate, but honestly, that was the only misdemeanour. We changed into indoor shoes on arrival and each of us had a shoe bag hanging from our cloakroom peg."
Lorna Newman

"First of all I went to Wyndham Lodge in Spring Grove when I was six. Then mother was visited by Father Green, a rather eccentric Catholic Priest, and he asked, "where does Joan go to school"? When she told him he said, "had you thought about sending her to Gumley"? Her reply was, "yes but we can't afford five guineas a term" and he said, *"I am sure that could be arranged"*, and so it was. It was a good school, at least I think it was better then than now. I quite enjoyed it." *Joan Temple*

"My memories of being a boarder span the last nine years of the boarding school to 1968. We had a special weekend uniform. Saturday mornings we used to go swimming. On weekends we also went for a long walk often along the Thames. We walked in pairs with one nun leading the way and another at the back to make sure we did not dodge into the local shops. However, this was often accomplished!" *Mary Coakley*

Spring Grove Central
"Our Head Mistress was Miss Bailey. She was lovely. There was the one large school, half for girls and half for boys. It had one large playground but half was for the girls the other for the boys." *Mrs. C. Inman*

Spring Grove Grammar
"On passing a scholarship I transferred aged 11 to what we called the Black and White School, where I stayed until 17 in 1939. The first headmaster was past retirement and useless. A new head Mr. Laurence Theodore Brown revolutionised the school - *I idolised him.* I was always in the football team and our coach was the history teacher who was Bernard Joy ex-Arsenal and England centre half." *Leslie Lees*

Isleworth Polytechnic (Spring Grove)
"This is where I went to evening classes for Pitman's shorthand and typing 1963-1965." *Mary Smith*

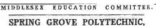

The Green School for Girls, London Road
Originating as a Sunday School, c1796, it carried on as an elementary school. A new educational climate saw transformation to a Secondary School for Girls for which Henry George, 7th Duke of Northumberland, erected a new building on his own land at Busch Corner. This opened 16th January 1906.

The Green School ladies

"The new in-take, of which I was one in 1928, had no form room the first year so each morning we gathered at Busch Corner and, accompanied by a teacher, set off for the ten minute walk to the 'Little School' in Park Road. This consisted of one huge, lofty room and a small room which two six formers used for prep. They wore their hair up with coiled plaits called 'earphones' and seemed very grown up to us. The heating consisted of a coke boiler which a lovely old lady, Mrs. Greenaway, attended to. She always wore a hat and skirts down to her ankles. She left a pan of water on the stove every morning, in which to *heat our milk for elevenses*, for which we paid one penny a glass."

"All school uniform items had to be purchased from Perks of Hounslow:- a black velour hat with green silk band bearing the badge of Middlesex County embroidered in red; green blazer and box pleat tunic, long sleeved Viyella oatmeal blouse, green fleecy lined knickers with a pocket for a handkerchief, black woollen stockings kept up with garters and black low heeled

1934

The Green School Summer uniform

shoes. We took off the tunics for gym, which we did in blouses and knickers, but wore the tunics for games and then came back to classes. No change of clothing or showers then!" *Grace Cousins*

"Our P.E. teacher, Miss Hains, encouraged good posture by presenting a House Cup. This was one of about a dozen awarded annually. She coached me for five years before I finally managed to swim - much to her delight. At Christmas we pupils looked forward to the staff pantomime. *It was quite a revelation!* " *Pauline Betts*

Marlborough Senior a mixed school, later became Marlborough Secondary for

Girls, and subsequently Marlborough Training Centre for pupils of 16+. The London Road building was demolished 1995.

"When I was there it was half boys, half girls – boys on the left, girls on the right. The playground was segregated too. First band I had – four fellows and me - we played

Marlborough sports day - 1949

80

for an old scholars' night at Marlborough, it was all ballroom dancing in those days. One waltz we got quicker and quicker I remember by the end people were *flying around the room*." *Ray Farnden*

"After the Town School I went to Marlborough leaving at age 14. The picture of the Tinder Box is about 1938. I was *understudy to the fairies*, and I don't know what happened, perhaps they didn't like being in the play, but they all went off sick on different nights and I ended up playing each of the parts, Gold, Silver and Bronze." *Kathleen McManus*

Marlborough senior school - 'Pygmalion' cast - 1959

The Marlborough cast of 'The Tinderbox' - circa 1938

"Pupils were divided into four houses, Caxton, Elgar, Van Gogh, Curie. We competed in various ways, sport, swimming, etc. All house points gained for good work, and lost for bad behaviour, were also counted up throughout the year. There was an award for the house which accumulated the most. On Sports Day the houses competed and we were all encouraged to cheer our own. Competition was seen as good for our development but if any girls booed the other teams, teachers would be down on them *like a ton of bricks*." Sportsmanship was very important." *Pam Strickland*

"We lobbied to be allowed to wear a short tunic or shorts for P.T. like girls at other schools, as we had to make do with awful navy knickers. The mistress in charge, Miss Gee, firmly but

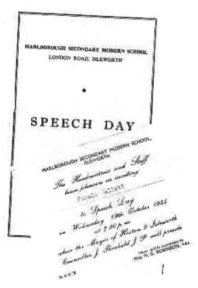

unsuccessfully, strove to convince us we looked better as we were. Needless to say her will prevailed." *Christine Diwell*

Smallberry Green School built in 1939 - a linocut by G. Small, 4B, 1949

Smallberry Green Senior School Opened 1939 it became in turn Smallberry Green Secondary Modern and Syon Upper School for Boys. Vacation of the London Road site started in 1979 and part of the grounds now houses Smallberry Green Primary School.

From a school of some four hundred boys, roughly half had a hand in production of this publication. A great deal of preparatory work was done out of school time. Mr. Liddicoat, senior history master, has been the chief guide in selection and lines of research. Ordinary school materials have been used and the whole book arranged and designed to look as attractive and tasteful as possible. Historical Isleworth 1949

"I was not good at metal work. One day when making a bracket, I had it in the vice and the teacher told me "you don't do it like that". But as he went to show me the right way the hammer I was holding *came down and hit him on the thumb*.

He turned round and hit me – he had massive hands - it sent me flying across the classroom. I wasn't hurt it was just a shock." *Len Evans*

"Because it was the end of the war time there were no major competitions between schools for the football team, although we did play a few inter-school games." *Paul Turner*

Isleworth Grammar School, Ridgeway Road
Originally it was an off-shoot of the old Blue School foundation. From September 1906, when the Middlesex County Council assumed control, to April 1952 it was known as Isleworth County. The name Isleworth Grammar was confirmed in 1954 and, on amalgamation with Syon School in 1979, it became Isleworth & Syon Boys' School.

"After going to Isleworth Town, I went to the County School in St. John's Road – the playing field was where Copper Mill Drive is now. It moved to Ridgeway Road, just at the beginning of the War. I was in the top form so we had to help move everything. As I was in the chemistry class I helped move all the laboratory, and then Mr. Hitler *went and dropped a bomb on it* - the end nearest to where the County Courts are now – but it only affected a small bit of the school, the rest was usable."
Bert Kendall

Oaklands, Woodlands Road
A special needs school taking pupils aged 11-19 with a whole range of handicaps both physical and learning difficulties, some severe. Opened 1971, it had previously been a centre for the visually impaired.

"To give you an idea, in one class 10 of the 11 children are in wheelchairs. There's an emphasis on one to one care – a maximum capacity for 72 children involves 15 teachers and 40 back up staff. Two new classrooms were built recently but still more are needed. They are currently trying to put in a small all weather football pitch but the sports day has to be held on the WERFA (Woodlands Estate Resident Freeholders Association) recreation grounds because of lack of space." *Brian Pett*

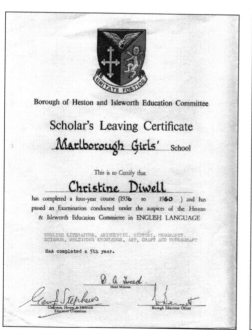

'Romeo and Juliet' performed in 1947 in The Green School annexe, St. John's Road

Worple Road pupils were divided into four houses - St. Patrick, St. Andrew, St. David and St. George. This painting of St. David once hung with that of the other saints in the school hall

chapter fourteen
The Working Day

The Undertaker
Charles Mayger, undertaker, funeral furnisher and carriage proprietor, est. 1850, operated from Alma House, North Street. The firm, later carried on by his sons, closed in 1960.

Kidd's Flour Mill
"The mill employed many of the men folk. Flour was ground there, stacked in bags and left by barges. Further along on the opposite side of the road was a large building with walls a yard thick, which was evidently a storage place of some sort. There was a long funnel or chute attached to this building from the mill, coming overhead across the road. You walked along beneath and could hear, high above your head, the corn rushing through." *Laura Hubbard*

"My grandfather worked there, he was what they called a dresser, a stone dresser. They'd grind a new surface on the big stones used in the mill." *Josie Best*

"My father was a labourer, and my elder brother a loader on the vans." *Mrs. E. Woodland*

Clock Mender and Winder
"I estimate that cycling to and from Syon House, attending to the clocks and enjoying a refreshment break in the servants' quarter took up a morning." *Tommy White*

Gardener at Syon
In midsummer 1920 Mr. Francis Farnden arrived to take up a temporary, three day, appointment as relief stable foreman. Today, nearly 48 years later, he is one of the longest serving members of the gardening staff. His change from horses to horticulture

started when he exercised horses by harnessing them up to a mower to cut the lawns. These covered 48 acres and took three weeks to complete. It was not long before he was working in the gardens full time. He now works part time looking after the lawns in front of the house and Great Conservatory, and also assists the Gardening Centre. Mr. Farnden's services to horticulture were recently recognised by the Royal Horticultural Society, who

Francis Farnden, gardener at Syon

awarded him their long service medal. Garden Centre News, Winter 1967/8

Coates Printing Works

Ron Self operating the linotype

"I've been here since 1946. In the early days there were three employees as well as my brother Ron, father and me. Mother did the folding and collating. There was no linotype machine at first though we got one soon after. Eric Winter was here 40 years from when he left school at 14. He worked in the composing room as we did quite a lot of hand work then. My present helper's been with me 23 years since he left school aged 16. We used to produce some nine magazines a month, as well as invoices for firms like Watneys and Hercules Engineering. I've just carried out an order for 100 invoices but it's rare nowadays. The bulk of the work is draw tickets – some two million a year." *Charlie Self*

River Trades

"When I left school I went to work for Thames Steam Tug and Lighterage Company, a very dirty job that involved tarring barges and *making tea for everyone* who worked there, for which I was paid £1.2s.6d per week."
Eric Brown

"One notable feature was the yellow vans *carrying huge squares of ice* from Lower Square Wharf and the workers were all Italians." *Mrs. E. Woodland*

86

"The men that worked the wharf, they was always covered in black, like the Black and White Minstrel Show. They worked in this awful dust in the warehouses loading lorries. I think the carbon was taken up to Firestones for tyres." *Don Hughes*

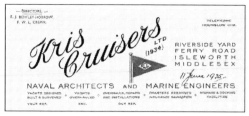

Gillette

"I worked at Gillette until 1982, starting 1949 – my first job as a cost accountant was to do costings for Toni Perms as they'd recently started producing them. Then I moved into production control in the razor manufacturing section. It

Good mornings begin with

Gillette

...the sharpest edge in the world!

was one of the first firms not to work Saturday mornings, had a subsidised canteen and they gave children's allowances. There was an active social side. Next to the canteen was a large hall used for dances, *plays by their own theatre group*, cinema shows, and always a Christmas party for employees' children." *Dennis Bignall*

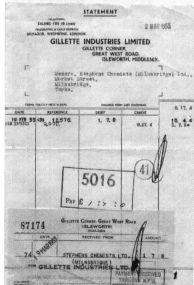

The construction of the S.W. London sewage works

Mogden Sewage Treatment Works

"Raw sludge was purified by a digestive process in enclosed tanks. Enough power was produced to drive all the machinery on the works, on occasions with some over to supply the grid. The sludge smelt earthy and was sold as Morganic – manure. There was never any trouble selling it on a commercial scale, *farmers took it away in lorry loads*. It was also bagged up for allotment holders. The site covers some 75 acres, there used to be some 250 employees – it's all automated now, making many redundant. I was a chemist, worked in the laboratory taking samples, checking processes. Had to know everything that was going on. It was interesting work I enjoyed my 31 years there from 1952." *Bert Kendall*

St. Christopher's Service Station, 120-130 St. John's Road

"An agent for Regent Petroleum told me of this vacant service station in 1965. It was run down and filthy, only doing petrol sales and had no staff, just a 'holding' person from Regent. There were three petrol pumps under a gantry alongside the pavement. I arranged the contract, took the premises and started to *scrape up the grease*, remove the oil and make it presentable. Three years later the old lock-up buildings were demolished and new tanks installed as were new pumps, this time away from the pavement." *Michael Becker*

On the Newspapers

Half the family worked at the brewery, the other on newspapers. My father worked for the Evening Standard. So did I. And I was at Isleworth for it at one point because every area had a depot so I came to the one here. In those days we would get the newspapers from the train at Isleworth station and distribute them. We all had our own 'manor' and were responsible for distribution and collection of money. I remember all the old newsagents, Rushton's, Miller's and Simpson's. Simpson had an old green van. He was a character - would take the papers off of us, take them round the hospital and back to his shop. *Always had a roll-up in his mouth*." *Rob Dickers*

Post Office Savings Bank at Osterley Park

"I worked for the Post Office Savings Bank at Osterley Park around 1950. The building was I think some sort of temporary pre-fab. There was a large work force and a group of us decided to entertain the other employees. We sang all the songs of the day, *Chattanooga Chu Chu* and the like." *Kathleen McManus*

Entertainment - Post Office Savings Bank style

Dye Makers and other trades in Worton Road
Mr. and Mrs. William Digby Hicks-Usher lived at Holly Lodge; in the grounds a kind of red dye used for colouring doorsteps was manufactured.

"My father was a dyemaker, worked for Mr. Hicks-Usher. I used to take his dinner down to him in a basket because he couldn't get home at lunch time. In 1928 the road was flooded and *they had to take us by boat*, rowing us down and back again." *Rosemary Chatfield*

In the mid-1950s Bert Bartholomew's company Richard Barland & Co occupied the lower part of the front of No. 292 and manufactured central heating ducts etc. On the top storey was Star Shop Fitters. Joined at the back was a factory occupied by Willesden Plating Limited. Today, Bert Bartholomew's son, Ron, is a well known local Councillor.

RICHARD BARLAND
& CO. LTD.

Ventilation - Dust Extraction and Air Conditioning - Sheet Metal Work - Prefabrication - All Types of Welding

WORTON WORKS
292 WORTON ROAD
ISLEWORTH - MIDDX.

Tel. HOU 0934 (Later to be changed to ISL 4548)

"Aged 17, I got a job as dolly boy at Trollope & Colls. They made large cement pipes. A 'dolly' was a piece of metal 14 inches by three. I was required to crawl into the steel drum, push the rivet through a previously made hole, then hold it in place with a dolly whilst a man outside banged away to seal the rivet. The echoing noise was deafening and the vibration on my arm painful. *This went on all day long* and I stuck it out for six months." *Ken Norman*

"Trollope & Colls must have moved in on the orchard site at the back of our house when I was still at the Town School.

TROLLOPE & COLLS LTD.
for
PRECAST CONCRETE
PIPES
MANHOLES
GULLIES
INSPECTION CHAMBERS
CABLE DUCTS
ETC.

WORTON ROAD,
ISLEWORTH

They were public contractors, builders who manufactured concrete drainage pipes at the works, using metal moulds. When complete they would leave the pipes to 'mature', row upon row all over the place, of various sizes from small drainage ones, to sewers six to eight feet in diameter. Then they'd take them away in their own fleet of lorries. It was a very busy site." *Bert Kendall*

The old and the new: wire braiding machines at the modern factory of Ormiston Wire Ltd

Established over 200 years ago Ormiston Wire Limited, now under the leadership of sixth generation Mark Ormiston, maintains the motto Any Kind of Wire – all types, ferrous and non-ferrous can be supplied in any size or length, or can be re-drawn, braided, according to specific instructions.

"The firm moved from Ealing in 1989, to give a more efficient workspace. Several of our 12 employees came with us but five live locally - *our oldest is 95* as we don't have a retirement age. Last year we were delighted to be one of only nine companies in the country to gain The Queen's Award for Enterprise, for sustainable development." *Mark Ormiston*

West Middlesex Hospital
"I was a Staff Nurse on Casualty and Outpatients from 1956-60 and joined the Hospital Players. All members whatever their grades/classification were equal. Two three act plays were produced annually. Our dress rehearsals were performed to an audience of walking patients, otherwise the audience was friends and relations." *Lorna Newman*

"I was born in West Middlesex Hospital 1948, just before the National Health Service came in. My mother was a nurse at the hospital, she came up from Swansea to do her training. After she married she gave up nursing, then I came along." *Ian Macklearn*

"I worked at West Middlesex Hospital as a cleaner. It was hard work. Nearly everyone worked at either the brewery or the hospital." *Theresa Turner*

"When I went there to work 1949-50, it had around 998 beds. We had a medical director, he was a Scotsman called Mr. Galloway, very honourable, a surgeon. He ran the hospital. His office door was always open for anybody whether a senior consultant or junior secretary. In a way you had to get to know him, he was a little brusque, but he was very good. A good surgeon and he ran things like clockwork." *Joan 'Molly' Brown*

A & F Pears

"My dad worked for Pears for about 35 years. I can remember him bringing home from the lab some of the products, soap, face powder, lipsticks, perfume. He worked as an alcohol recoverer. To make the transparent soap translucent, alcohol was put in, but had to be extracted before the end of the process or it would have burned people's skin." *Kath Howard*

Diana Sadler wearing the Pears factory uniform whilst on war work in 1914

In 1914 Pears was acquired by Lever Brother to become, in turn, part of the Unilever conglomerate.

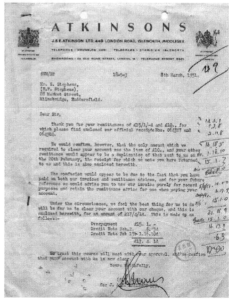

On the Land

"A Mr. Lewis had market gardens between the hospital and cemetery and even though I was a schoolgirl I got work there. My first day was spent picking onions for which I earned one shilling and six pence. *As a treat I bought fish and chips* for three pence and gave my mum some money." *Mary Huxley*

"A common sight was the women coming from the market gardens, all with their coarse sack aprons pinned up behind them. How those women must have worked." *Mrs. E.Woodland*

Film Industry

Worton Hall was one of the first film production centres established in England, and in recent years extensive additions have been made to its accommodation and equipment. Thomason's Directory 1939

And other employers...

Watney's or Isleworth Ales.	ISLEWORTH Bottled Beers.
Reid's Stout. Combe's Brown Ales.	These well-known Beers are sent out from the Brewery in absolutely perfect condition and represent
These well-known brands of Bottled Beers have achieved a high reputation entirely by their **Superior Quality**. Always in sparkling and fresh condition. Obtainable at all Watney and Isleworth Licensed Houses, and Off Licenses in the district.	TO-DAY'S BEST VALUE.

ISLEWORTH PALE ALE - 8d. Per PINT
Sparkling and Refreshing

ISLEWORTH STOUT - 1/3 Per QUART.
Pleasant, Nourishing and Sustaining

ISLEWORTH BOTTLED BEER.

Bear facts

From the flowers to the hive, from the hives to you, honey in its purest form. Unrivalled quality in ½-lb and 1-lb jars. The finest and purest procurable.

Bear Brand *Honey*

L. GARVIN & CO. LTD.

Branch: THE BEAR HONEY CO. LTD.

ISLEWORTH, MIDDX. Telephone: Hounslow 3433

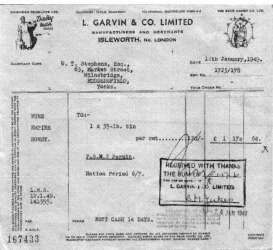

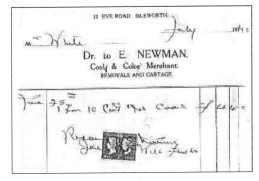

GUARANTEE

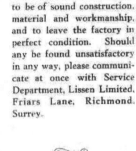**A**LL LISSENOLA In-
struments are guaranteed
to be of sound construction,
material and workmanship,
and to leave the factory in
perfect condition. Should
any be found unsatisfactory
in any way, please communi-
cate at once with Service
Department, Lissen Limited,
Friars Lane, Richmond,
Surrey.

LISSEN LTD.

WORPLE ROAD
ISLEWORTH
MIDDLESEX

FLUIDRIVE ENGINEERING CO.LTD.

TELEPHONE ISLEWORTH (12)
          6 LINES
TELEX 24107

DIRECTORS: JOHN F PERRY A.M.I.Mech E, A.M.I.E.E.
            ANTONY VICKERS B.SC., M.I.Mech E
            LEONARD WATSON F.C.I.S., F.A.C.C.A
            A. L. J. SQUIRE
            E. C. FARRER M.C.A.M.I.Mech E.
            W. H. R. JAMES M.A.
            JOHN RAYMOND, M.I.E.C.

YOUR REF
OUR REF   AEG/MK.

TELEGRAMS FLUIDRIVE, ISLEWORTH, TELEX
           AND
           HYDYNAMIC, ISLEWORTH, TELEX
           (TELEX ANSWER BACK) FLUIDRIVE)

FLUIDRIVE WORKS,
WORTON ROAD,
ISLEWORTH, MIDDX.

15th June, 1962.

M Lockyer Builders

Tel: 020 8758 2211
Fax: 020 8847 0886
Mob: 07885 332 505
Email: lockyer.crown@btclick.com

Unit 1
Waterside Business Centre
Railshead Road
Isleworth
Middlesex   TW7 7BY

The North Street junction
with Swan Street

chapter fifteen
Days of Change

In 1904 the new farmhouse was built behind the stables completing the series of buildings known as Worton Farm. It was one of the best planned houses I have ever seen, an ideal home. Also it was one of the first in the district to have electricity and the telephone; the telephone number was Hounslow 10. Jessie Lobjoit Collins, Key of the Fields

"I went down St. John's Road on the way to school. There were some very nice Georgian houses at the bottom, they just fell into disrepair. At the top of South Street were some nice Georgian houses and also facing the Gumley playing field in the Twickenham Road." *Joan Temple*

As a matter of historical interest it may be as well to place on record the following statement concerning the erection of the War Memorial:

	Receipts	*Expenses*
Contributions	*£ 582.12.6*	
Monument		*£ 460.7. 9*
Interest	*£ 32.15.1*	
Clock		*£ 98.0.0*
Printing		*£ 18.10.9*
Opening ceremony		*£ 9.3.11*
Advertising/sundries		*£ 15.5.2*
Balance presented to		
Isleworth Philanthropic Society		*£ 14.00*
	£ 615.7.7d	**£ 615.7.7d**

Yours faithfully, John Weathers, Hon. Secretary,   *27th January 1923*

"I remember when Brantwood Avenue, Cleveland Road, Chestnut Grove and others were all orchards or market gardens, and Mogden Lane was just a muddy path." *Albert Turner, Sundial Parish Magazine*

"Opposite Syon's Lion Gates is a garden - once part of a field surrounded by a white fence in which sheep grazed. We children were taken there for some celebration and told in a speech by Councillor Snowy Fielder it was going to be a park with swings and slides, and there would be a rose garden for the elderly. *It did all happen.*" *Mary Huxley*

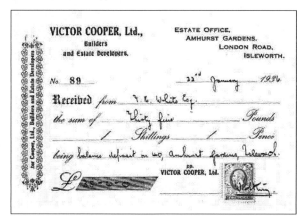

"The houses in Amhurst Gardens were built on the site of old orchards and some trees were left in the gardens – mixed apple and pears. *I've dug up many pieces of clay pipes.* Now far fewer people use their gardens to grow vegetables." *Leslie Wrangles*

"When my much loved Sunday school teacher, Miss Perry, was ill my friend and I telephoned her from the 'phone box that stood by Quaker Lane. Making a phone call was *quite an event* for me." *Pauline Betts*

With so much that is historical falling before development and progress, it seems a fitting opportunity to place on record – before too late – some of Isleworth's importance in other years, before its resurgence into Industrial Isleworth. Foreword to Historical Isleworth, printed 1949

South Street demolition

"There was a big red brick building where the park is now in North Street. We used to shin over the wall. The allotment holders didn't like it and *chased us away*." *Peter Farmer*

"I can recall a nasty accident late in the '50s. A man was knocking an old building down and I think he was killed." *Sheila Hance*

South Street undergoes redevelopment

"In North Street there was a Carmelite convent – now the grounds are called Silver Hall. I remember the Worple estate being built - the ground at that time was all market gardens, but it was so beautiful, a mass of fruit blossom in spring." *Mrs. E. Woodland*

"There used to be huge bonfires – *people burnt anything*, three piece suites, tables, chairs – on the wasteland bombsite before the Hartland Road estate was built. We used to call it 'The Gunge'." *Audrey Morris*

"One of the changes was the loss of the poppies. They were the size roughly of the inside of a saucer and in colour a very rich, very dark, red. Must have come from one of the gardens, might have been where the British Legion is now. Gradually the bomb site spaces were built over, and as they went, so did the poppies." *Lionel Watson*

"After the War we came back to live in prefabricated bungalows on the area where

Newly built Swann Court - named after Harold Swann, Town Clerk

97

Hartham Road is now, people don't seem to remember them. *They were made of asbestos* – cold, but we had a coal fire." *Peter Farmer*

"On my first day of going to Spring Grove Grammar School I saw they were clearing the

The conversion of the former Odeon cinema

ground next door on the London Road to build the Odeon Cinema." *Leslie Lees*

"Where you go down Church Street at the ground by the bridge, there used to be parts of little houses there, lovely cottages - daffodils still come up, they must have been in somebody's garden once." *Mary Crickmore*

"We lived in Bridge Road; the first houses built in Hounslow or Isleworth after the end of the War. My father was looking for somewhere to live. He heard on the grapevine new houses were to be built and went down to look. There was a plot of four semi-detached and he very quickly put a deposit on one. So I think they moved in around 1946, and lived there for 35 years." *Ian Macklearn*

"We watched our house in Arnold Crescent being built, visiting every weekend, standing in a field of mud. There was a tragic accident when Ivy Bridge estate went up – a staircase collapsed and a worker was killed. The South West Isolation Hospital stood where Tesco is, and now they are rebuilding the bridge over the Duke of Northumberland's river." *Barbara Friend*

Old Isleworth Plan Ready – Early Start Urged – By-pass, Shops, Health Centre, Bus Station.
The comprehensive development plan for Old Isleworth was approved by the County Council on Wednesday. It includes plans to more than double the present residential acreage, build a shopping centre, re-site the Blue School and extend the Richmond Road northwards to Busch Corner. Newspaper cutting 27th June 1952

"During the 1950-60s, they re-built Isleworth, new for old, largely putting flats in South

Street roughly where the forge was when I was a boy. Re-built unkindly to my mind, I sang of it to my poor old mum "Little boxes" - like the pop song - when she'd have loved to have lived in one of them. Our little box was still the one or two rooms in the old house by Busch Corner. And all Church Street nearly got re-built." *Lionel Watson*

"In the early '60s people were moving out of the area, the quest was to get a house with a bathroom, with an indoor toilet instead of outside. My first recollection of going into new houses was around Shrewsbury Walk. *I got friendly with a Cypriot lad*, went to his flat above the barbers. I was so impressed with the brightness of the walls and light switches." *Don Hughes*

"It was headmistress Mrs. Nicholson who acknowledged the limitations of the old building and began the planning for the new. The foundation stone was laid and hymns sung to the accompaniment of a recorder group, and at Whitsun 1961 the Blue School moved proudly into its new premises. Infant classes on the ground floor, juniors on two floors in a separate block, toilets indoors, a kitchen, a staff room – *such unprecedented luxury!*" *Arthur Spikins*

"My husband worked for the company that built Lynton Close

– before that it was apple and pear orchards owned by Tommy Mann. We used to tour round the site trying to decide which plot we wanted. We moved in 1959, ending up with a corner house, bordered one side by Redlees Park - then allotments - with Mogden at the back, the ground just sloped up to the works then. The trees that are there now came later." *Kit Turner*

"When we moved to Worple Road in 1968 the house belonged to the council, it had no heating or internal toilet, the only water supply was in the kitchen. Three years on, it was decided something should be done about the whole area. The authorities were remarkably forward looking and consulted through visiting every house, having meetings, questionnaires and surveys, to establish what people who lived there wanted. Overwhelmingly people wanted to *retain and improve the houses*, not demolish and re-build." *Shirley Bascran*

"Ours was the only non-white household when I came here from India in 1972. One of my earliest memories is of being approached in the street by an elderly white lady whom I had noticed staring at me previously. I grew anxious, fearing a torrent of verbal racist abuse. Instead, the woman, marvelling at my colourful sari, said it was an honour and privilege to meet *a lovely young Indian princess*. Such encounters are typical of my generally positive experiences in Isleworth." *Harbans Kaur Singh*

1983 saw the start of a consultation programme to set out some of the choices for re-development of Old Isleworth, and discuss proposals put forward by Speyhawk Land & Estates Limited. 'The Options' occasioned much controversy, some battles were won and some lost.

The Chairman
and Directors of
Speyhawk public limited company
request the pleasure of the company of

Mr & Mrs D. Gillett

at the unveiling ceremony by the Rt. Hon. Sir Ian Gilmour, Bt. M.P.
of the recently renovated Glossop Memorial Drinking Fountain
on Monday 10th September 1990
at Northumberland House, Lower Square, Old Isleworth, Middlesex
at 6.00pm

R.S.V.P.
Sebastian Blakemore
Speyhawk investments plc
Osprey House, Lower Square,
Old Isleworth, Middlesex TW7 6BQ
081-560 2161

"Taking his courage in both hands, my husband Ken asked the Chairman of the Heritage of London Trust for a donation - the result was £2,000. It took five years of triumphs, and one or two disasters, to raise the necessary £10,000 but in 1990 work to restore the Glossop Memorial began." *Helen Cooper*

"We were the first to move into the new development and the removal people were unable to put our furniture in because the painters were still here. Speyhawk arranged for us to stay the night at an hotel in Richmond. A lunch was held at their headquarters, John Day House; the Mayor presided and our photos appeared in the paper with him handing us the keys." *Daphne Peters*

Lower Square undergoes a transformation

"They were still building in Church Street when we arrived. Two big furniture vans stood outside our new house while they asked us to "wait a few days". This being impossible, we stacked the furniture in the garage and lodged in the rooms still being plastered. We could see the river from the house at first but always knew that offices would be built up opposite. Existing residents did not find it easy to adjust to the idea of houses and offices replacing the 'dockland' area. The new construction was a complete, and not always welcome, change of use." *John Ray*

Pimple Shop is no Isleworth Beauty Spot
A South Street shop has been refused an extension because "it already looks like a pimple on a pig's behind" according to one Isleworth South Ward Councillor. The plan was to build a single storey extension to create office space and a bedroom. *Hounslow Chronicle, July 1996*

"When the Day Care Centre was to be closed some 30 or so of us went along to the Civic Centre. There was one very rowdy group, who would not shut up despite pleas from the lady Mayor. Eventually we were all deprived of hearing the discussion because the public was turned out of the gallery." *Alan Cooke*

"We lived in Linkfield Road, bought the house in the 1950s for £1,800. *It sold a few months ago for £190,000.*" Sid & Molly Stoddart

"The Clock Tower Memorial was unveiled in 1922 to honour local men who died in the 1st World War. By the 1990s exposure to the elements left its mark so, through the efforts of a small group inspired by Rosemary Coomber, donations large and small totalling £22,068.39 were raised. After many hiccups and delays, restoration was completed in time for the 2002 Remembrance Day Service." *Kate Williamson*

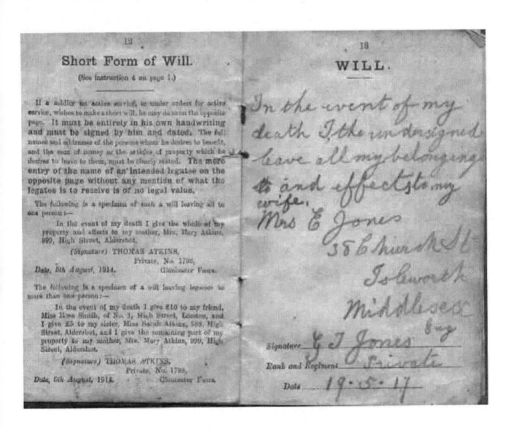

chapter sixteen
Down by the Riverside

The Floods

"With water splashing all over my legs I dashed back down the centre of Church Street shouting at the top of my voice to warn others the flood was already at the doors. Luckily everyone heard and proceeded madly to roll up carpets and move as much as possible upstairs." *Eileen Sheridan*

"A flood in the 1960s was very bad. We had a roach come into the hallway. When I told my husband the water was flooding into the front room he said *"save the wine"* – he used to make his own wine, which was stored in dustbins." *Theresa Turner*

"Mother-in-law, during one of her visits, was marooned upstairs with all the excess furniture and it was quite a hilarious performance as we sat her on rolled up carpets and slid her downstairs." *Eileen Sheridan*

Four years' ago Church Street residents were informed nos. 36-52 would have their river walls raised and strengthened and those with gardens would have them banked up to the new height so that there was not an abrupt 'step up'. *Sundial Parish Magazine, 1979*

Taking a dip

"My dad told me *not to do it*, but I learned to swim in the Thames. He could always smell the river on me when I got home!" *Mary Huxley*

"Some other lads and me were paddling about in the murky half

L. GARVIN & Co LD

MERCHANTS

LONDON · ISLEWORTH

·· COPENHAGEN ··

tide waters when there was a commotion. One of the others, with his bare hands, had caught a roach or dace, full grown, *under the hull of the big iron barges* that used to be moored there." *Lionel Watson*

River Trade

"A common sight was Dutch merchant seamen in clogs in South Street on leave from their boats which were unloading and reloading in Lion Wharf up until the mid to late thirties." *Tom Black*

"It was always so busy with boats coming in from London and the continent. The Dutch sailors used to come round Isleworth in their *clogs and funny little hats*. There were always barges by the London Apprentice, children used to dive off them and go swimming." *Josie Best*

"I remember the old crane in Lion Wharf, the original one. We'd go there with barrows to get coal, they would sell it loose by the one hundredweight and we would lug it all the way back to Spring Grove." *John Benn*

Lion Wharf

"My wife's father was foreman of Lion Wharf. When we married we lived with her family on the wharf in Shrewsbury House – it was big, we only had the upper part, the downstairs was offices. *You could see the barges outside*, unloading the coal and timber. Eventually we had to get out because Charringtons took over part of the wharf for oil and said they wanted the place for offices." *Ray Farnden*

Isleworth Rowing Club

"I came to live in Church Street in

1952 - a feature indelibly implanted in me is the sight of the Belgian, Dutch and German coasters that plied between the wharves here and ports across the channel. Five cranes would swing to and fro loading and unloading all types of cargo." *Eileen Sheridan*

WINNERS OF THE ISLEWORTH SKIFF MARATHON.
F. DILL, E. C. YOUNG, F. PEARSON.

Messing About in Boats
"I missed some afternoon school sessions, my chum Tinny Williams had a boat and we used to mess about on the river." *John Beal*

"In my days in service at 59 Church Street I saw so much of the young men who belonged to the Rowing Club, out every Sunday morning in their smart white flannels and straw hats, all crowding down to Mr. Finn's boathouse. We seemed to get such long summers then and the boats were out in plenty all day and evenings." *Mrs. E. Woodland*

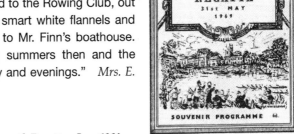

"As a lad I spent school holidays with Graham. His father worked at Waite's boathouse. Mr. Waite was a Waterman. He had a lifebelt from the Mauritania in the boathouse and a stuffed seal, *which had been caught in the Thames*. Sometimes we lads helped by sweeping up and were allowed to take a boat out as a reward." *Leslie Wrangles*

Isleworth Regatta - June 1964

ISLEWORTH FERRY

OLD ISLEWORTH
SYON HOUSE & PARK
PARK ROAD
CHURCH
CHURCH ST
FERRY
KEW
RIVERSIDE WALK
KEW GARDENS
LONDON APPRENTICE
RIVER THAMES
OLD DEER PARK
RICHMOND

Open Late May Bank Holiday
until the end of September

Weekends & Bank Holidays
10.00am - 6.00pm

Special offer for visitors
to Kew Gardens
£1 OFF Adult entry for
Ferry Passengers

Revival of the Isleworth Regatta was proclaimed a huge success last year, and it was unanimously agreed this event should take place annually. Rowing and canoeing courses have been slightly changed to give the spectators a complete view of the races whilst still retaining the ancient and beautiful scenic background.   Isleworth Regatta Souvenir Programme, 27th July 1963

"While at school I was part of a rowing pair and won a shield at the Isleworth Regatta. Later I became a member of the Regatta committee and used to design the programme covers." *Frank Winterborne*

The Ferry
Isleworth Church ferry dates from Henry VIII's time. It closed 1939 to re-open at weekends after the War until 1953. Subsequently revived it ran until around 1970. Ferryman, Mr Dargon, sold it to Speyhawk in the 1980s when it operated during some summer months. 14th July 1994 saw Jonathan Radgick acquiring the rights at auction for £6,000, together with a 1930s classic mahogany boat. But, again, the service was short lived.

"It cost one penny on the ferry. We didn't go across it to Kew Gardens often, it was too far to walk. The names of the ferrymen I remember are Mr. Finn, Mr. Sims and Con Dargon – he had a place by the ferry where you could get tea, coffee and ice cream. It was good there. His daughter still lives in the area – we keep in touch." *Theresa Turner*

"It would run to the Richmond side and you paid a penny or whatever it was. One summer when the river was very low the ferry stopped because people were just *walking across the river*. I happened to be down there with some other children. We were highly delighted because we got across." *Joan 'Molly' Brown*

Wild Life
"We would go on long walks by the river especially on the other side over the Lock Bridge and along to Kew Gardens. I also swam in the river when about age 12, and we would spend hours looking for wildlife in the stream called the Minnie HaHa." *Pam Strickland*

"We enjoyed watching a pair of Egyptian geese standing on the banks grooming their beautiful feathers, their amber eyes set in a dark mask-like patch. They stood together on their pink legs against the dark foreshore, the sun picking them out at the water's edge." *Eileen Sheridan*

The Ait

"After coming to live here I became interested in the bird life, took a course in wild bird recognition, and also became involved in conservation of the Ait, another activity that has

A regular visitor - The Egyptian Goose

been richly rewarding over the years. Even though I've since had to move, I am still on the Ait Management Committee." *John Ray*

A vista board was proposed by the Ait Management Committee - Thames Water agreed to pay for the design, while The Town Wharf provided a site on its balcony overlooking the Ait and financed making of the board. On Friday 19th November it was finally unveiled in the presence of the Mayor and invited guests. Sundial Parish Magazine, 1999

"We weren't allowed to but we went to the Ait, walking across when the tide was out. There was also a small island by the London Apprentice." *Peter Farmer*

"It was my first visit to the island despite having lived here 53 years – it was nice to be in a totally wild, unspoilt area. I'd never seen cormorants perched on branches so close before." *Keith Knight*

Fishing

"From a boy I have always loved the river, fishing there, later teaching my three sons to fish. I still enjoy a trip down memory lane to the riverfront at the Apprentice." *Eric Brown*

"Where the mill pool is, we used to go over the wall – there were steps at the side, we would fish when the tide came in." *Peter Farmer*

Making music on the Cathja

"One afternoon I bunked off school and went fishing, my passion. Walking home was my headmaster. On seeing me he said "Don't tell me you were on the first bus because I was, but if you *catch a fish in ten minutes* I will not split on you". I caught one in two and a half minutes!"
Leslie Lees

The Cathja
"Summer 2000 six professional entertainers walked their way along the Thames Path stopping off to sing with local communities. On a beautiful sunny day they called at the old Dutch barge moored opposite the Ait, where below deck people stressed out by modern living relax by working with wood. On this idyllic day, helped by some Green School pupils, all work gave way to a joyful session of music."
Christine Diwell

The Lock Bridge
"We had a junior school trip to the Lock Bridge to see how it worked. Men would manually turn big handles to lift the sluice gates, at the same time large weights would go down to counter balance them. The Lockmaster's house was by the side of the

Half Lock Bridge

bridge; it had a beautiful garden. Now the sluice gates are managed automatically. There were lots of pleasure boats going up and down the river. *I once saw a Viking ship* by the Lock Bridge." *Pam Strickland*

And other memories...

"The noise of the water going through the sluice gates at the Mill Basin helped you to go to sleep at night." *Theresa Turner*

"I'd viewed the house and liked it but the owner thought I should see round the area. At the rear access into Harcourt Close, paling fences surrounded the shrubs by the new houses there. It did not look good. However we walked through Silverhall Park, past the almshouses, down to the river. This tipped the balance. I'd found my home. I knew I could be happy here." *Pam Booth*

"Price was what prompted me to move here. It was quite simple – we couldn't afford Richmond or Twickenham! I'm very pleased we did because, apart from anything else, we get the view across the river to Richmond." *Arthur Horwood*

Isleworth Riverside was designated a Conservation Area in 1972, the largest such area in the London Borough of Hounslow.

Isleworth Riverside

Conservation Area 11

London Borough of Hounslow
Date of Designation 11th November 1972

Hounslow

Lion Wharf

HIGH WATER AT WAITE'S
BOATHOUSE.
(We are indebted to Messrs. J. S. White & Son
for the use of their copyright.)

SEPTEMBER.

A tide table from 1928

A linocut by D. Walker, 3B Smallberry Green School - 1949

BOATYARDS - OLD ISLEWORTH

The ISLEWORTH SOCIETY

President: The Rt. Hon. The LORD GILMOUR of CRAIGMILLAR

chapter seventeen
the Isleworth Society

Established around 1960, as the Friends of Old Isleworth, the Society's aim then, as now, is to promote interest in, preserve and enhance the unique character of the area, as well as support community projects.

To commemorate 30 years' service on the Isleworth Society committee 88 year old Helen Cooper planted a cherry tree alongside the Glossop Memorial in South Street.
Brentford Chiswick & Isleworth Times, 14th December 2001

An early leaflet by the Friends reminded residents there's always been a local cause to be fought - a 1635 proposal to put a lime kiln near the river at Isleworth was opposed because it was "too fair a seat for so foul an employment". During its formative days, in the 1960s, the group found itself fighting to save a tree-lined stretch of the riverside, overlooking the Ait, from being spoiled by the erection of oil tanks.

The Friends continued in their role as a local watchdog. By 1975 Heritage Year, with the annual membership fee set at 25p, it aimed to provide residents with an opportunity to "say what you think is necessary for the good of the community".

One core activity became the monitoring of planning applications – never more so than during the mid-1980s when a wind of change swept through the area and Speyhawk, having purchased the properties

MILLSTREAM

a newsletter from the   Number 1
Society of Friends of Old Isleworth   October 1977

In the attempt to put together the first issue of "Millstream", we present a miscellany of topics to interest and, we hope, bring you along to the Society meetings to participate. At the moment there is no particular format for the newsletter or personnel to produce it. Your help and suggestions are invited. Don't forget: we need any items - anecdotes - problems - humour, which you feel are suitable for inclusion in a future issue of "Millstream".
The immediate aim is to provide for Members and Friends a source of up to date information, with the accent on Society action and progress, whilst stimulating other meetings, discussions and activities among members.

Parish Church, Isleworth.

Friends of Old Isleworth

of H. Taylor (Isleworth) Ltd, submitted plans for extensive re-development. Even local schoolchildren were involved in overseeing the proposals, when they were asked to provide their opinions on Speyhawk's ideas, with prizes allocated for the best entries. And so a new name for the Friends, Isleworth Civic Trust, came about.

Friendship was always part of the Isleworth way. Getting things done while keeping a smile on everyone's face. In 1986, the society celebrated its Silver Jubilee, by holding an innovative 'Public' Committee Meeting, with a wide-ranging agenda, allowing everyone to "have a say". Equally important, in terms of retaining a feeling of togetherness was a buffet held at Syon House, by kind permission of the then President, His Grace the Duke of Northumberland.

ISLEWORTH CIVIC TRUST

25th ANNUAL GENERAL MEETING
& SILVER JUBILEE BUFFET

To be held at SYON HOUSE

by kind permission of His Grace the Duke of Northumberland KG GCVO TD PC JP FRS

FRIDAY 11th APRIL 1986 at 7 pm

Tour of the House

Ticket £7.50   Dress: Lounge Suit

"The 25th anniversary celebration took place at Syon in April – a buffet supper and tour of the house. I remember it being so cold we ate with our coats on." *Andrea Cameron*

A revised constitution in 1992 found the group widening its scope and changing its name to the Isleworth Society. To take the fight where needed, links with others have always been embraced, FHANG (Federation of Heathrow Aircraft Noise Groups), the Isleworth Ait Management Committee, Police and Environment Forums, being among the various causes. And if one had a title that hardly tripped off the tongue – The Duke of Northumberland's River Awareness Campaign Joint Working Party (DNRACJWP to its friends!) - it did culminate in providing a sign-posted nature walk and accompanying booklet.

CIVIC TRUST

Caring for Places where People Live and Work

CERTIFICATE OF REGISTRATION

1991-2

This is to certify that

THE ISLEWORTH CIVIC TRUST

is a Society Registered with the Civic Trust and is included in the UK Register of Local Amenity Societies for 1991-2

Martin Bradshaw
Director

"The good and the great of Isleworth were all on the committee – Tom Girtin, Michael Penty, Archdeacon Hayward. Later, Gareth Hoskins came along and the outlook of the society widened. Before this it concentrated on the Church Street area. It has broadened considerably since that time." *Pam Booth*

Achievements have been both great and small – from opposition to a plant-

drooped Arab dhow draped over the London Apprentice's doorway, to establishment of The Green and a pathway across, graffiti clean-ups, a riverside seat and numerous other improvements. The many notable successes to which it has given support include, Grade II listing of Isleworth Public Hall and creation of further Conservation Areas – all by the unstinting work of committee members, sponsors and the membership as a whole.

P.C. Hollis draws the raffle at the Osterley Fair, 2002

"Once, over lunch, I asked how I could help get involved in local things. By chance my companion was just giving up being membership secretary of the Isleworth Society. Eleven years later I was about to give up doing this job myself." *Pam Booth*

But social activities have always been and remain an important feature, ranging from wine and cheese evenings, garden parties, talks, quiz nights and puzzles for children to fairs, festivals, walks and visits. The first Carols in Lower Square celebration, with its now traditional tree, lights, mulled wine and free mince pies, took place nine years ago. Hundreds of those who care about Isleworth have taken part in them all.

If you, too, feel the same way about a place that has been dubbed 'the prettiest village along the Thames' then call the membership secretary on 0208 568 1337 or Chairman 0208 560 1129.

Eileen Sheridan congratulates the winning team of the Initiative Quiz

113

DISCOVER THE TREASURES
OF
OLD ISLEWORTH

DOMESDAY
TO
MILLENNIUM

SUNDAY 23RD JULY

JOIN THE EXCITING TEAM GAME
STARTING
AT
**ALL SAINTS CHURCH
ISLEWORTH**
11: 30 A.M.

TEAMS OF CHILDREN AGE 6-11 MUST BE ACCOMPANIED BY 1 ADULT
TEAMS OF " BIG CHILDREN" (ADULTS) CAN ALSO TAKE PART
ENTRY FEE £2.00 PER TEAM - END WITH REFRESHMENTS AT APPROX. 1:30

Isleworth
Remembered

Whether you're 8 or 80, we'd like to hear your impressions of Isleworth

The Isleworth Society invites everyone to join us in the Public Hall for a nine-day celebration of our local life.

Whatever your age, come and share your memories with our members and tell us what you like about living here. Everyone has a story to tell, and the best will be compiled into a new local history book.

This fascinating and important project is sponsored by the Rugby Football Union.

also

Walks, talks & exhibition

Saturday 4th to Sunday 12th May
Isleworth Public Hall, South Street
Full programme overleaf

Carols in the Square

Once again this popular gathering will take place at
the Lower Square, Isleworth at 7.30 p.m. on

Thursday **12th** December

This is a change to the previously published date

114